M000010326

The (Smart Guide) to
MARKETING

TOP MARKETING IDEAS

How to become the
SMARTEST PERSON in the room

(Jack Gaskell's "Smart Guide" Series - **BOOK #1**)

Jack Gaskell

Professional Value Books, Inc.—North Palm Beach, FL 33408

https://www.TheEngineersResource.com

The Smart Guide to Marketing

This publication is designed to provide accurate and authoritative information in regard to the subject matter covered. It's sold with the understanding that the publisher is not engaged in rendering legal, accounting, or other professional service. If legal advice or other expert assistance is required, the services of a competent professional person should be sought.

International Standard Book Numbers (ISBN)

Softcover:	978-0-9964197-6-5
Hardcover:	978-0-9964197-4-1
E-Book:	978-0-9964197-3-4

Proof Reader: AZ Editing (Ginny Glass)
Book Interior Designer: JERA Publishing (Stephanie Anderson)
Cover Designer: JERA Publishing (Jason Orr)

Publisher: Professional Value Books, Inc.
110 Shore Court, Unit 304, North Palm Beach, FL 33408
https://www.TheEngineersResource.com

Library of Congress Control Number: 2020904020

DEDICATION

To all of us who never got all As but became successful by being savvy and applying much hard work and effort.

ACKNOWLEDGMENT

The author wishes to acknowledge his thanks to the many wonderful acquaintances who read the prepublication copy of this book and later posted reviews on Amazon. Your help did much to contribute to the book's success.

ABOUT THE AUTHOR

John D. Gaskell is a retired consulting engineer.

He was president of Gaskell Associates Consulting Engineers, now a division of Thielsch Engineering, Inc. Jack is a graduate of Wentworth Institute, with an associate's degree in electrical engineering technology, and the College of Engineering at the University of Rhode Island, with a bachelor of science degree in electrical engineering.

Jack was a member of the following professional organizations: Rhode Island Society of Professional Engineers, Providence Engineering Society, Electrical League of Rhode Island, Illuminating Engineering Society of North America, National Electromagnetic Field Testing Association, and the National Academy of Forensic Engineers.

He is a past president of the Rhode Island Society of Professional Engineers, founding president of the Rhode Island chapter of the Illuminating Engineering Society, past director of the Electrical League of Rhode Island, and past chairman of the Electrical Code Sub-Committee of the Rhode Island Building Code Standards Committee.

Jack was honored by being selected Engineer of the Year by the Rhode Island Society of Professional Engineers; Man of the Year by the Electrical League of

Rhode Island; and was awarded the Providence Engineering Society's Freeman Award in recognition of major achievements in engineering.

He spends winters at his home in North Palm Beach, Florida, enjoying the warm weather and losing at the game of pool. Summers are spent at his home in Warwick, Rhode Island, enjoying his children, grandchildren, and many great friends. Jack also has written three other books: *The Complete Guide to Consulting Engineering*; *The Outline Guide to Consulting Engineering*; and *The Consulting Engineer's Guidebook*.

GUARANTEE

The publisher is so convinced that you'll be 100 percent satisfied with this book that we provide a full money-back, no-questions-asked guarantee, provided that you purchased the book from the website: https://www.TheEngineersResource.com

Just notify the publisher at Professional Value Books, Inc., 110 Shore Court, Unit 304, North Palm Beach, FL 33408.

DISCLAIMER

The author, Jack Gaskell (John D. Gaskell), is a retired/inactive/no-longer-licensed engineer. He feels qualified to tell you how he started and managed his consulting engineering practice and to give marketing advice. But he is not an attorney, accountant, insurance expert, or any other kind of business professional, and can only give general guidance, which should always be confirmed by an attorney or other appropriate professionals before proceeding. He has expended considerable effort in the preparation of his books, articles, and blogs. He believes, to the best of his knowledge, that the information contained therein is accurate. Nothing should be construed as legal advice, and he offers his apologies, in advance, for the inevitable blunders.

CONTENTS

SHORT READ

For best memory retention the author recommend that you read this book in no longer than 45 minute segments (22-32 pages). Also, your own notes of key issues will encourage your memory to retain information. You are encouraged to include page numbers in your notes for easy reference. Extra pages are provided at the end of the print version of the book for that purpose.

Re-reading a second time will increase retention by at least 20 percent. Good luck and I wish you much continues success.

CHAPTER 1

INTRODUCTION

I'm an electrical engineer and a graduate of the College of Engineering at the University of Rhode Island. With this one statement, you're likely thinking that I must be really smart. That's one of the reasons you should get the best education that's within your means.

When I was in college, I worked summers selling encyclopedias door-to-door and, by living with my parents, saved my entire tuition. Unfortunately, with today's educational costs, this is no longer possible.

Some of my classmates never studied and got all As and Bs. (I still hate those guys.) I studied day and night and seldom got a grade above a C. and I graduated in the bottom half of my class. However, I was savvy, and I knew how to market myself and my professional practice, and within ten years, many people thought that I was "the smartest person in the room" (You are what you are thought to be) and also that my engineering practice therefore must be the best. If you pursue my advice, you can also gain that regard.

If you're truly smart, you may not need my advice. But if you're a mere mortal, you might benefit from it.

See how to plan for your career. Understand that your career must be lucrative enough to support you and a family, not restrict where you can live, and not require odd hours or excessive travel. Grasp how attending local meeting of organizations in your industry will help you to get known. Learn how to start a contact list and how to make it more than just a list of names. Realize how easy it is to become an officer of any organization and perceive the value of that credential. Comprehend how to get yourself nominated for prestigious awards that will make your resume stand out. Glean how to choose the profession or business that is right for you. Find out how to prepare your business announcement, letterhead, business cards, and brochure distinct from those of your competitors.

Realize how public speaking opportunities are *free* publicity. Learn why you need to start a notebook to record anything that you might need again and discover why spending time each week reading about new topics in your field, business trends, and current affairs will enhance your reputation. Learn what a *white paper* is and how it will be useful in promoting your reputation and that of your company. Realize that people judge your intelligence at your first meeting. Understand why you should encourage the other person to speak and discover what a *conversation statement* is and why you need one.

Understand why collecting business cards and starting a contact list will help your reputation and realize why you should expand your mailing list to include all the players in your industry. Ascertain how to select topics for your articles and how to submit them to magazines. Learn how to design, print, and distribute reprints of your articles. Finally see why almost any kind of speaking engagement enhances your image and credibility.

If you truly want to accomplish these goals, turn this page.

CHAPTER 2

GETTING STARTED RIGHT

INTRODUCTION

See how to plan for your career. Understand that your career must be lucrative enough to support you and a family, not restrict where you can live, and not require odd hours or excessive travel. Find out how spending a day with someone in the field that interests you will help you to decide. Realize if owning a business is right for you. Learn how to find out the median salaries of your career choices. Comprehend how to conduct a job search and prepare for the interview.

How to Make a Career Choice

At the high school level, students should consider career options. Don't choose a career just because it sounds like fun. Make sure that it will be lucrative enough to support you and a family, won't restrict where you can live, and won't require odd hours or excessive travel. I have a friend whose daughter became a marine biologist and later found out that it qualified her to shovel seal poop.

Before spending four years of your life and your parents' hard-earned money, you should be reasonably sure that your chosen options are right for you. I recommend "shadowing" somebody in the fields that interest you. If you don't know someone, use the internet. Make a phone call and explain that you're a high school student interested in becoming an _____ and would like to speak to an _____. Explain to the _____ that you would like to come to his or her office and observe a typical day. Very few people would turn down that kind of request, and it might turn into a summer internship or a job after graduation. If you're unsure of your specific career choice, call _____ of various specialties to try and gain an understanding of what their jobs entail. Spending time with several _____ would broaden your perceptive.

In my case, my father was an electrician. I helped him with side jobs and grew up with an interest in electricity. I chose to take an academic vocational course in high school, radio, television, and industrial electronics, with the goal of becoming a TV repair person. (Do you know anyone, today who's making a living repairing TVs?)

In my senior year of high school, two of my classmates decided to go to Wentworth Institute in Boston, Massachusetts, for associate's degrees in electrical engineering; so I applied and was accepted. When my two years at Wentworth were almost complete, a friend in my class told me that he was going to a four-year college for a bachelor of science degree in electrical engineering while getting almost two years of credit for his associate's degree. So I applied at the University of Rhode Island and was accepted—but with no credits for the two years at Wentworth. However, low in-state tuition and the ability to commute from home made this the only realistic option for me.

Instead of stumbling your way through six years to become an _____, plan ahead and do it in four years. In high school, take a college prep course that's strong in the subjects related to your area of interest.

When selecting a college, make sure that it's accredited in your area of specialty.

Make a List of Benefits and Drawbacks

- your interests/lack of interest
- your skills/lack of the required skills
- challenging/easy
- varied/repetitive
- lucrative/adequate/inadequate
- free time/busy schedule
- cyclical industry/steady demand
- time spent inside/outside/both
- travel opportunities/too much travel/no travel requirements
- offers opportunity to own a business/not
- require immediate actions/allows time for thoughtful decisions
- low stress/high stress

- high demand/low demand
- puts you in an adversarial position/not adversarial
- deadline pressure/leisurely pace
- profitably pressure/nonprofit
- periods of too little or too much work/steady work
- limits where you can live/no limit
- high cost and time for education and internship/low cost and time

DO YOU WANT TO OWN A BUSINESS?

Advantages

- You have a much higher earning potential.
- You have pride of ownership.
- You get the benefits of being the boss.
- You get to make all the final decisions.
- You can't get laid-off.
- You get to keep the profits.
- You can pick and choose the most appealing tasks to personally handle and assign the others to your staff.
- You can pursue the most interesting and profitable projects/ products/clients.
- You spend time socializing with clients and potential clients.
- If you're successful and hire an able staff, you'll have a valuable asset to sell when it comes time for your retirement.

Disadvantages

- Stress—There's always stress when owning a business. Some people thrive on it; others wilt. You need to decide if the benefits/advantages outweigh the drawbacks/disadvantages.
- Be prepared to make sacrifices. When I was new in business as a consulting engineer and still operating alone, work slowed down, and my wife and I decided to take a quick driving vacation to Canada. At the last minute, I got a call from my biggest client announcing that

he had just promised a client of his to provide a redesign that had to be delivered in one week. It was no fun having to go out to the car to break the bad news to my wife and two small children.

- You make the firing decisions. This is particularly hard during the holiday season.
- The losses are all yours. On average, I made at least three times more compensation than my fellow engineering classmates, but during one recession, I lost more than my salary for three years in a row.
- Employees. The biggest headache in running any business is managing human resources. Often, employees don't get along with each other or with the clients, and sometimes, they don't even care about the success of the company that employs them. Regardless, before you know it, you may be responsible for thirty or more mouths to feed. That is an awesome and burdensome responsibility.

Making a Choice

Other than a marriage choice, choosing a career is your most important life choice. If you're still undecided, I recommend that you go to the website: https://www.bls.gov/ooh/. This is the *Occupational Outlook Handbook* by the US Bureau of Labor Statistics. It has a wealth of information regarding career choices. First, select an occupational group that interests you. Then, see a list of occupations in that group including job descriptions, entry-level educational requirements, as well as recent median pay levels. Next select a career choice and see details.

My Recommendation

Only you can make this important life decision. But I recommend the following if you have the interest and skills:

- Choose to be a professional: doctor, lawyer, engineer, architect, accountant, and the like. When people learn that you're a professional, they immediately assume that you're smart. You may have never gotten any grade higher than a C; you may have graduated last in your graduating class; and you may have had to take your licensure exam four times before passing. But you're perceived to be smart because you're a professional, and potential clients will tend to choose your practice or business

- Choose a profession that will allow you to operate your own business. If you operate your own business, you'll have all the advantages described above.

My Start

As with education, I kind of stumbled into consulting engineering. In my senior year in electrical engineering at URI (University of Rhode Island), I happened to have lunch with a classmate who told me of an interesting summer job that he had working for a consulting engineer. I asked, "What is a consulting engineer?" He told me that his job entailed drafting for a licensed electrical Professional Engineer who provided consulting services to architects.

This accidental conversation set me on a path to becoming a consulting engineer. I sent a resume to each of the three electrical engineers listed in the local Yellow Pages and to several of the local architects. One of the architectural firms was utilizing an electrical engineer who was consulting to them on an hourly basis. He was reviewing the plans prepared by one of the staff architects and then preparing the specifications for bidding. This electrical engineer was approaching retirement, so they hired me to learn from him and succeed him as their in-house electrical engineer upon his retirement.

Fortunately for me, this electrical engineer, John W. King, PE, was one of the most knowledgeable and highly respected engineers in the State of Rhode Island. John started his career in the electrical industry as an electrician and later taught electricity to returning WWII veterans' at a vocational school. He then worked as an electrical inspector, and when a local architect needed help with the electrical design of a complicated project, the architect called on John, thus starting his career as an electrical engineer. Later, when the state required licensing of engineers, he was granted PE registration without an engineering degree and without an examination because of his experience and reputation. He was even appointed by the governor to serve on the Board of Registration of Professional Engineers from 1964 to 1975.

At some point, John opened up his own engineering office, providing services to many different architects and private clients (colleges, hospitals, building owners, etc.). Eventually, he became partners with a mechanical engineer.

When I introduced myself to Mr. King, he said, "Oh yes, my replacement." I don't remember my startled response, but we soon became good friends. It now reminds me of Thomas Jefferson's reply when he was presented as US ambassador to France: "I am merely Mr. Franklin's successor; no one could replace Mr. Franklin."

I worked for the architectural firm (while being trained by Mr. King) for about a year and a half. At that point, John and his partner notified the firm that John no longer had the time to consult to them on an hourly basis. Eventually, it was agreed that John and his partner would consult to them on a fee basis (as is standard in the industry), and I became John's assistant as an employee of John's firm. When the partnership later broke up, John decided to retire. My wife and I invited John and his wife to dinner and convinced him to join me in a new partnership with me providing the capital.

My father cosigned a small loan, and we worked in John's dining room for two years. In the meantime, I became a PE (a licensed Professional Engineer), and when John turned seventy years old, his wife convinced him to retire while I opened my own practice. John even gave me the drafting tables and other equipment. I called my company Gaskell Associates Consulting Engineers, and John let me use the words *Formerly J. W. King Associates* in my Yellow Page advertisement.

GETTING EXPERIENCE

Once you're a graduate in your chosen field, the first step is to get a job that will give you exceptional experience and to qualify you to eventually take a licensure exam, if required.

The Job Search

Depending on the job market at the time of your graduation, you may not have a wide range of job choices. But if you get a job unrelated to your goals, it's unlikely to lead to the success that you desire. You may have to consider commuting to a larger city to find work in your field.

First, prepare a resume, which, at this point, will only include your education and your summer job, if it involved your chosen career. But your summer job as a lifeguard won't impress a prospective employer. Include praiseworthy accomplishments, like being an Eagle Scout. Mention interests concerning your career, but certainly don't state an interest in eventually opening your own competing firm/business.

Make a list of related businesses in your area. Try to find a website for each to learn a little about them. Next, print your resume on nice paper and deliver it to each business on your list. Don't mail it.

Dress for success. Men should wear a suit or sport coat and tie. Women should wear a sweater and black dress pants or a blazer and skirt. A suit and bow tie worked best for me. Explain that you're a recent (specialty) graduate and would like to speak with the manager/president/chief engineer (whatever applies in your case). If they ask why, reply, "I'm seeking advice and will only take a few minutes." If they say he or she is busy, reply, "That's ok, I can wait."

If all else fails, ask the receptionist to present a copy of your resume and ask for the person's business card. If it's a good-size company, provide a second copy of your resume for the personnel department. If you don't hear back within a week, call the person to verify that he received your resume and to inquire about job openings. Prepare a list of questions and have a copy ready for each call with spaces for the answers:

- Did you receive my resume?
- Are there any entry level openings?
- Are any openings likely in the near future? If so, when?
- Can you recommend competitors who might be hiring?
- Do you have any advice for a young person just starting out?
- Can I come in to your office and observe a typical day? (An eight-hour job interview.)

Send a letter or email thanking them for taking your call and for the advice. (Include another copy of your resume.)

If you don't quickly get a job, stop back to see the same people. Their needs can change in just a few weeks. Consider bringing a box of chocolates, pastries or flowers for the receptionist who said that the person that you wanted to see was too busy to see you.

The Interview
Be prepared.

- If you're responding to an employment posting, make a list of the skills desired so that you're prepared to discuss and relate them to your training and education. Don't be concerned if you don't have all the qualifications listed. There may be an entry-level position available.

- Make a list of five skills and qualifications of yours that you can share during the interview.
- Go to the company's website to learn more about the company so that you'll be better prepared for questions, like "What interests you about our company?"
- Make a list of likely questions that you may be asked and prepare answers: Why should I hire you? Is there anything about the job or the company that I haven't told you? What are your career goals in the next five years, and how will you achieve them? What are your salary requirements?
- Make a list of questions about the job and the company, and bring up your questions if the interviewer doesn't offer the information.
- Ask if you can meet someone in a similar position and the person who will be your immediate supervisor.
- Ask about the skills that you'll be learning and applying in the available position, and access their relevance to your future goals. For example, assume that you're an electrical engineer and wish to open a practice designing electrical systems for buildings. A position as a lighting designer won't teach you the diversity of other skills needed.
- Try not to look like a deer in the headlights; practice in front of a mirror. Listen carefully and don't be afraid to take notes during the interview. Bring extra copies of your resume, including a list of references. Also, bring your list of questions, a pad (in a folio), and a pen. Don't bring a drink or chew gum, and turn your cell phone off.
- Send the interviewer a thank-you note or email.

You may have to widen your job-search area, but with persistence, you'll eventually get a job in your chosen field.

Start the Job Right

Once you have a job, do your best to be *exceptional*. Arrive early and leave late. Start a notebook to record information, such as formulas, code rules, contacts, and anything that you might need again. My notebook was a three-ring binder; yours will be your computer or iPad. (See chapter 5—"Your Notebook.")

Ask a lot of questions, but avoid the same question a second time—consult your notebook.

I soon learned that Mr. King could never answer a question with a yes or a no. His answers always came with a story and a long explanation. This was often frustrating when we were up against a deadline. But it taught me related things, helped me to remember the answers, and gave me an understanding of the why.

Fill your notebook with knowledge.

It's critically important that you stay up to date. This involves weekly reading, including magazines in your industry and in your specialty, code updates and interpretations, business trends, and current affairs. This will aid you in your present job and help your future endeavors to thrive and prosper in any economy. Dedicate at least four hours a week to this task. Always have something with you to read. Don't waste time waiting for doctors while reading outdated health-care magazines.

Start writing *white papers*. A white paper is a report or guide to help readers to understand an issue. (See chapter 6—"White Papers.")

OUTLINE GUIDE

- **Plan ahead:** Don't stumble into your career. Plan for it.

- **Your career choice:** Should be lucrative enough to support you and a family, not restrict where you can live, and not require odd hours or excessive travel.

- **Shadow**: Spend a day with someone in the field that interests you.

- **Owning a business:** Make a list of advantages and disadvantages
    - Advantages: Making all the final decisions; never being laid-off; keeping all the profits; and being able to sell an asset upon retirement.
    - Disadvantages: Personal and family sacrifices; difficulty of dealing with employees and acceptance of any losses.

- **Visit the website** https://www.bls.gov/ooh/: The *Occupational Outlook Handbook* by the US Bureau of Labor Statistics.

- **My recommendation:** Choose to be a professional and own your own business.

- **Your job search:** Prepare a resume; check websites of potential employers; dress for success; and make follow-up calls.

- **Prepare for your interview:** Make a list of your skills, a list of anticipated questions with answers, and a list of your questions. Also, send a thank-you email.

- **Start the job right:** Be exceptional, start a notebook, and start writing white papers. (See chapters 5 and 6.)

What people are saying:

Included are more than 100 marketing methods. + I can't believe what great marketing ideas are included. + This book focuses on the top marketing ideas ever used. + These are the best small business tools for any profession. + I ordered two more as gift marketing ideas for my children. + This is one of the best sales and marketing books ever written. + This is a list of sales tools that I can choose from in the future.

CHAPTER 3

BECOMING KNOWN AND GAINING CREDENTIALS

INTRODUCTION

Grasp how attending local meeting of organizations in your industry will help you to become known. Learn how to start a contact list and how to make it more than just a list of names. Realize how easy it is to become an officer of any organization and perceive the value of that credential. Comprehend how to get yourself nominated for prestigious awards that will make your resume stand out. Perceive how savings, good credit, and banking contacts will be the key to starting your own business.

Becoming Known

I was a nobody; I came from a blue-collar family and had never even seen the inside of a country club. But I was savvy enough to realize that I needed to start building an outstanding reputation and more credentials.

As soon as you graduate, start attending meetings of local organizations in your field of interest. Even if you don't have a job yet, it will give you an opportunity to meet people in your industry. These contacts might help you get a job or help you in other ways.

Here you'll meet the players in your profession/industry, people who will be your colleagues, future competitors, or future employees. In most cases, you don't even need to join to attend meetings. Try to get on the local mailing list so that you'll be notified of meetings. Now most organizations have websites were meeting notices are posted. Most are usually evening dinner meetings with a guest speaker.

As a newly graduated engineer, I joined several organizations and attended meetings of the following:

- The Rhode Island Society of Professional Engineers (RISPE)
- Providence Engineering Society (PES)
- Electrical League of Rhode Island(ELRI)
- Illuminating Engineering Society of North America (IES)

Rhode Islanders initially had to drive fifty miles to attend meetings of the Boston IES chapter. But we had local meetings after a group of us formed the RI chapter of the IES, of which, I'm proud to say, I was the founding president. (Since I was only twenty-nine and new in the business, I was very pleased that my colleagues chose me as the first president. It was not until years later that I learned that they had previously been turned down by all my more experienced competitors.)

At meetings, collect business cards from those that you want to get to know. Start making a contact list, including both business and personal information. You'll form a quicker and closer friendship if you can remember that he or she has an interest in baseball and has a three-year-old daughter named Michelle.

Gaining Credentials

Initially, my resume included membership in the above-listed organizations. My next goal was to become a board member of RISPE. I asked the local president if there were any committee openings; there are always openings. I chose to become publications committee chairman, which qualified me to attend monthly board meetings, meet the leaders, and be seen and known. Soon, I met the nominating committee chairmen. After our friendship was cemented, I expressed interest in being on the board, and I became Treasurer the following year (most nominees run unopposed). That put me on the ladder, and I became RISPE president in four years. After my presidency, I nominated one of the recent past presidents for the Engineer of the Year award; not surprisingly, in a few years, he nominated me.

I don't mean to imply that all this was easy; it took a lot of hard work. But, with determination and effort, you can establish credentials that will eventually distinguish you from your competitors. The important lesson here is that it doesn't just happen—you make it happen.

Public Speaking Experience

Most professionals and leaders in business attend gatherings where their credentials are reveled. As a consulting engineer, I frequently attend interview meetings, where building committees select architects and engineers for their projects. I have watched many of my colleagues talk about their college degree, and then all that they had was a list of past projects. In addition, I could refer to the following:

> I am a past president of the Rhode Island Society of Professional Engineers, the founding president of the Rhode Island chapter of the Illuminating Engineering Society, past director of the Electrical League of Rhode Island, and chairman of the Electrical Code Sub-Committee of the Rhode Island Building Code Standards Committee.

> I have written numerous articles for national technical publications and have been a guest speaker at the National Conference on Harmonics and Power Quality in Philadelphia.

> I was honored by being selected Engineer of the Year by the Rhode Island Society of Professional Engineers and Man of the Year by the Electrical League of Rhode Island.

> I am particularly proud of being a recipient of the Providence Engineering Society's Freeman Award. This award was established for the purpose of recognizing major achievements in engineering.

I wasn't bragging; I was applying for a job.

If you want to be successful, don't be afraid to build yourself up. Fortunately, your work as an officer of professional organizations will give you many opportunities to hone your skills as a public speaker. In your career, you'll be required to speak before both small and large groups. At this point, I am reminded of one of my least auspicious experiences as a public speaker.

During my first or second year in practice, I was hired to do a light-emissions study. This was in conjunction with an environmental impact study relating to the proposed expansion of a local airport. I don't know if I was chosen because my resume included "member of IES" or because I was too new to properly quote a fee for such an unusual project. In any case, I visited the airport at night, under varying weather conditions, and (with a light meter) measured the light produced from the approach lights. My final conclusion was that the amount of light was less than the light emitted by a full moon and, therefore, had no significant impact on the environment. I submitted my report to the environmental firm that had hired me, and it was accepted.

After about six months, the environmental firm called me and asked me to attend a public hearing at the City Hall to answer questions, if any. I reread my report, and with a copy, I sat down in front with the other members of our team. The remaining five hundred seats were occupied by very angry neighbors, with many more standing around the perimeter of the room. The head of the environmental firm was called to the podium and, after a few introductory remarks, said, "And now I would like to call our electrical engineer, Jack Gaskell, to the podium to present the light emissions portion of our report." I considered running for the door, but I didn't think I could make it down the center aisle.

I rose with wobbly legs and walked to the podium with my report in hand. When the heckling from the crowd quieted down a bit, I said, "I have to start out by apologizing; it was my understanding that I was here to answer questions (if any) and, therefore, did not prepare a presentation. But I have a copy of my report and will paraphrase it for you." I opened my report and stumbled through. When I was finished, everyone booed, and I took my seat. Even after all of these years, I still break out in a sweat when I think of that public hearing.

The lesson here is always be prepared to make a presentation.

Start to Save Money

Most financially successful people own their own business or professional practice. This means they are going to need equity to start or to buy-in.

It's important to start saving as soon as you're working unless you have a benefactor or can find a rich person to adopt you. If you're living from one paycheck to the next, you'll never be your own boss. If you (or your spouse) get deep into debt or ruin your credit, forget about owning your own business. Don't live above (or up to) your means. Get as much overtime as you can, or consider a part-time job. Postpone that trip or new car until you have fulfilled your dream. Your goal should be to save between 10 and 20 percent of your income, including your spouse's income.

Establish Relations with Financial Institutions

When starting or buying a business, most people need to supplement their savings with borrowed money. Start establishing financial contacts before you need to borrow for a new business. If you plan to have partners, it's best for each of you to establish a relationship at different institutions. A main branch of each is usually the best choice. Also, avoid the institution that holds your mortgage to avoid the possible seizure of personal funds if your new business fails.

OUTLINE GUIDE

- **Become known:** Attend meetings of local industry organizations. Here you'll meet the players in your profession/industry, people who will be your colleagues, future competitors, or future employees.

- **Start a contact list:** Including both business and personal information.

- **Become an officer:** Volunteer for committees and attend board meetings. Eventually, let it be known that you want to be an officer.

- **Win awards:** After you have been active in an organization, nominate another involved member for an award and they will later return the favor. Or have a mutual friend suggest it.

- **Start saving:** You'll need equity, good credit, and banking relations to start a business.

- **It doesn't just happen.** You make it happen.

What people are saying:

Included are more than 100 marketing methods. + I can't believe what great marketing ideas are included. + This book focuses on the top marketing ideas ever used. + These are the best small business tools for any profession. + I ordered two more as gift marketing ideas for my children. + This is one of the best sales and marketing books ever written. + This is a list of sales tools that I can choose from in the future.

CHAPTER 4

YOUR PROFESSIONAL PRACTICE OR BUSINESS

INTRODUCTION

How to choose the profession or business that's right for you was discussed in chapter 2—"Getting Started Right." This is one of the most important life choices that you'll ever make. Before actually starting a business of your own, reflect on your previous choices and make any needed adjustments, before proceeding further.

Next, you need to decide if you're going to be a generalist or have one or more specialties. If you're an electrical engineer with a license as a professional engineer, you could offer electrical engineering advice of any kind to the public, or specialize in systems for buildings, lighting, fire alarm systems, forensic investigations, and so on.

Whatever you decide, try to project a smart and professional image.

Find out how to prepare your business announcement, letterhead, business cards, and brochure distinct from those of your competitors.

Realize how public speaking opportunities are *free* publicity. Ascertain why notes of congratulations and thanks and an occasional party will help your practice grow.

General

I think that finding and keeping clients is the key to success. Most people are shy. Get over it!

While attending college, I worked two summers selling encyclopedias door-to-door. In the process, I gained confidence.

I am not suggesting a second job, but you do need to get over your timidity. Your activities described under "Becoming Known and Gaining Credentials" in chapter 3 should have provided many opportunities to meet new people and occasions for public speaking. If you followed my advice, you'll stand out.

Business Announcement

Your business announcement should look and feel like a wedding invitation, with fine paper (perhaps matching your letterhead) and have raised letters.

Letterhead

When I started my practice, I chose a nice cream-colored parchment. This type of paper is often used by long-established law firms. I had it printed with black, raised letters, and I think that it looked classy.

In the internet age, this may not be as important as it once was, but I recommend the following:

- Select an elegant paper.
- Don't skimp on the cost of paper.
- Avoid bright or strange colors.
- See the actual paper and feel it before printing.
- Print with raised lettering.
- Use a black script, but make sure that it's easy to read.
- Avoid logos; everyone else has them.
- Include company name, address, telephone and fax numbers, and web address.
- Print "second-sheet" stationery with only your company name at half size.

Other than your website, your stationery will be the first image most people will have of your company.

Business Cards

I used the same parchment as my letterhead.

Your business card should include the same information as your letterhead, plus your name, title, and specialty.

John D. Gaskell, PE, President
Electrical Engineer

Company Brochure

During my second or third week in business, I went to a job site meeting with a mechanical engineer who was also new in private practice. On the car seat, I found three pieces of paper stapled in the top left corner. It was his resume and a list of his projects. He proudly said, "That's my brochure." I didn't know anything about company brochures, but I knew that mine would look more professional.

My first brochure was a resume and a three-page list of past projects. It was enclosed in a thick blue 11x17 paper cover (folded in half) and printed with my letterhead and the words COMPANY BROCHURE in large letters.

My second brochure had padded black-leather covers made by a bookbinder. It had gold embossed lettering and included the name of the client (or potential client) also embossed on the cover. The pages were encased in plastic sleeves. Is anyone going to discard something with their name embossed prominently on the cover?

My third brochure was not as fancy, but it was more versatile. It was bound with flexible, glossy, and embossed black covers, and the pages were printed on my letterhead without sheet protectors. This was inserted in the front inside pocket of a 10x12 glossy folio. My company name was printed on the outside front of the folio, and my company description/resume was printed on the back. In the rear pocket of the folio, I inserted fillers that I had previously sent to my mailing list: published article (written by me), award announcements, announcements of new services that our firm was offering, and so on.

My fourth brochure was a mini-brochure: a single 8 1/2x14 parchment sheet folded in thirds. It was only used as a handout at events, like speaking engagements with numerous attendees, when it was too expensive to provide my normal brochure. See figure 4-1.

Your brochure may evolve over time. But, most importantly, make it something of which you're proud.

BROCHURE (1 OF 2)

Why Architects Choose Gaskell Associates, Ltd.:

We carefully coordinate the electrical systems with the architect and his other consultants. We have developed a detailed series of "coordination sheets" to assist in this regard.

We review our design with and seek "Letters of Approval" from the local electrical inspector, power company, telephone company and superintendent of fire alarms.

We provide fast "turnaround" on shop drawings. We also review shop drawings of all "equipment" for proper voltage, phase and power.

We make periodic site visits during construction. After each visit, we provide a typed "Field Report," indicating the progress of the electrical work in detail.

Why Facility Owners Choose Gaskell Associates, Ltd.:

Detailed electrical drawings and specifications provide a basis for fair and uniform competitive bids.

As Professional Engineers, we act independently on the client's behalf exercising professional judgment without being subjected to outside influences.

We take the time to evaluate alternatives that result in the design decisions that balance efficiency, construction cost, safety, life-cycle costs, long-term performance and quality. Gaskell Associates, Ltd. has the reputation for creative and economical solutions to difficult design problems.

Careful monitoring of the construction process assures that the owner gets what he paid for. Services include: detailed review of shop drawings, periodic progress reports, field coordination, and review of requisitions.

Gaskell Associates, Ltd. are the professionals to turn to for all your electrical engineering needs.

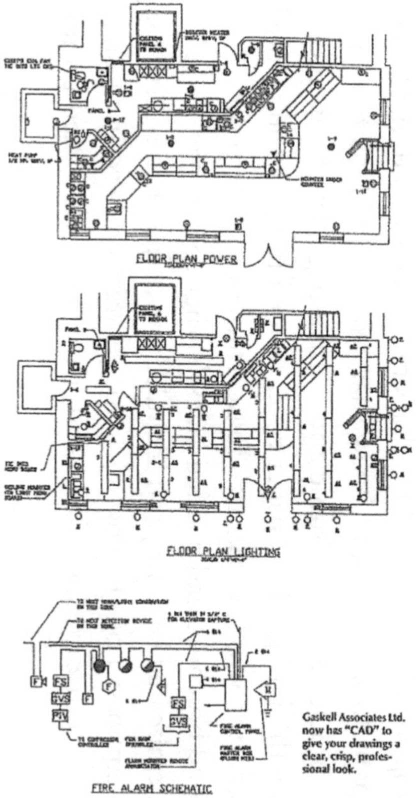

Gaskell Associates Ltd. now has "CAD" to give your drawings a clear, crisp, professional look.

GASKELL ASSOCIATES LTD.

CONSULTING ENGINEERS

300 Post Road
Warwick Rhode Island 02888

Tel. (401) 781-6696
Fax. (401) 467-9570

FIGURE 4-1

BROCHURE (2 OF 2)

Gaskell Associates, Ltd.

Gaskell Associates, Ltd. is a consulting engineering firm primarily involved with the design of electrical systems for buildings.

Our specialties include:

- Power Distribution Systems
- Emergency Power Systems
- High Voltage Power Distribution Systems
- Lighting Design (Interior, Exterior, Area and Roadway)
- Fire Alarm Systems
- Burglar Alarm Systems
- Communications Systems
- MATV and CCTV Systems
- Computer Power and Network Systems
- UPS and Power Conditioning Systems
- Feasibility Studies

In addition, we have developed a team of consultants to allow us to offer a full range of incidental services including: HVAC, plumbing, architectural, structural, and civil engineering.

Life-cycle-costing is a major element of our design effort and energy conservation is always considered. This results in a facility that is economical, efficient, functional, and easily maintained, as well as one that is aesthetically pleasing.

Gaskell Associates, Ltd. endeavors, at all times, to maintain its reputation for accuracy, attention to detail, and punctuality. We have executed engineering projects for almost every type of facility, including numerous renovations.

This engineering practice was established in 1971 by John D. Gaskell, P.E., electrical engineer. We now employ a staff of eleven.

John D. Gaskell, P.E.

Gaskell Associates, Ltd. is headed by John D. Gaskell, P.E. Jack is a graduate of Wentworth Institute, with an Associates degree in Electrical Engineering Technology, and the University of Rhode Island, with a Bachelor of Science degree in Electrical Engineering. He is a Registered Professional Engineer in Rhode Island, Massachusetts, Connecticut, New Hampshire, New York, New Jersey, Pennsylvania, and Florida.

Jack is a member of the following professional organizations: Rhode Island Society of Professional Engineers, Providence Engineering Society, International Association of Electrical Inspectors, Electrical League of Rhode Island, Illuminating Engineering Society, and the Institute of Electrical and Electronic Engineers.

He is a past president of the Rhdoe Island Society of Professional Engineers; past president of the Rhode Island Chapter of the Illuminating Engineering Society, past director of the Electrical League of Rhode Island; and past director of the Rhode Island Chapter of the International Association of Electrical Inspectors.

Jack writes the electrical specifications for our projects and provides executive project management. He has written several articles for national technical publications. His design of a one megawatt Uninterruptible Power System for Fleet National Bank's Operations Center won "first place" in a national design award competition.

Jack was recently honored by being selected "Engineer of the Year" by the Rhode Island Society of Professional Engineers.

Recent Clients

a i designs, inc., Pawtucket, Rhode Island
Gordon R. Archibald, Inc., Pawtucket, Rhode Island
Arris Design, Inc., Providence, Rhode Island
James Barnes, AIA, Providence, Rhode Island
Benefit Street Design, Inc., Providence, Rhode Island
Brown University, Providence, Rhode Island
Citizens Bank, Properties Dept., Providence, Rhode Island
The Coken Company, Providence, Rhode Island
Corporate Concepts, Warwick, Rhode Island
Cranston Housing Authority, Cranston, Rhode Island
Daughn/Salisbury, Inc., Providence, Rhode Island
Diocese of Providence, Providence, Rhode Island
Di Leonardo International, Inc., Warwick, Rhode Island
East Providence Housing Authority, East Providence, Rhode Island
Ekman, Arp and Snider, Warwick, Rhode Island
Charles B. Fink, A.I.A., Providence, Rhode Island
Fleet National Bank, Providence, Rhode Island
Garofalo Associates, Inc., Warwick, Rhode Island
Gates, Leighton & Associates, Inc., East Providence, Rhode Island
Gilbert & Maloney, Providence, Rhode Island
Irving B. Haynes & Associates, Providence, Rhode Island
The Hillier Group, Princeton, New Jersey
Kent Cruise & Partners, Providence, Rhode Island
Lamborghini and Feibelman, Providence, Rhode Island
Lincoln Housing Authority, Lincoln, Rhode Island
Long, Staats and Associates, Newport, Rhode Island
Americo Malzozzi, A.I.A., Providence, Rhode Island
George Morin Architects, Inc., Woonsocket, Rhode Island
Kevin S. Munroe - Architect, Wakefield, Rhode Island
Naval Underwater Systems Center, Newport, Rhode Island
O'Hearne Associates, Woonsocket, Rhode Island
Lee Pare & Associates, Inc., Providence, Rhode Island
City Of Pawtucket School Department, Pawtucket, Rhode Island
PPG Industries, Pittsburgh, Pennsylvania
Lombard J. Pozzi, A.I.A., Warren, Rhode Island
The Robinson Green Beretta Corp., (RGB), Providence, Rhode Island
Robinson, Myrick & Associates, Inc., Smithfield, Rhode Island
Roger Williams General Hospital, Providence, Rhode Island
The Ritchie Organization (TRO), Newton, Massachusetts
Rhode Island Department of Environmental Management
Rhode Island Department of Transportation
Rhode Island Division of Water Resources
Norton E. Salk, Architect, Cranston, Rhode Island
Raymond W. Schwab Associates, Inc., Peacedale, Rhode Island
St. Joseph Hospital, Fatima Unit, N. Providence, Rhode Island
St. Joseph Hospital, Providence Unit, Providence, Rhode Island
United States Navy, Newport, Rhode Island
Technical Materials, Inc., Lincoln, Rhode Island
Warren Housing Authority, Warren, Rhode Island
Warwick Housing Authority, Warwick, Rhode Island
City of Woonsocket, Planning Department, Woonsocket, RI
Womens Development Center, Providence, Rhode Island
Veteran's Medical Center, Providence, Rhode Island

FIGURE 4-1

Note Paper

Print notepaper (4x6) with "From the desk of (name and title)" at the top (example: From the desk of John D. Gaskell, PE, President) and with your company name, and your contact information at the bottom. Also, have some printed for your senior staff. It should be on the same paper as your letterhead. Attach it to anything that you mail to a client. It's much more classy than a blank piece of paper or a notepaper with a vendor's name on it. A personal, handwritten note on nice paper makes the right impression.

The more prevalent use of internet communications has made notepaper less relevant and less important. However, a handwritten note gets more attention and may be more appropriate for certain interactions.

Website

Much to my surprise, a professional firm's website has become one of the most active sources of new clients. Some new clients will go to your website because of a referral or because they have heard that a competitor of theirs does business with your firm. However, you'll find that many of your clients will find you while surfing the net.

Most importantly, your website should look professional. Do not try to design it yourself; hire an experienced professional. If you have a colleague who has a great website, ask about his website designer. Did the designer heed the client's wishes, and was working with him or her easy? Were they quick in constructing and delivering the site and in making requested updates? How are the hosting services?

Your website should have the following general features: be quick and easy to navigate, not produce any sound/audio, bear the same main headings on each page, be easily changed and updated, and have no blinking, spinning, or moving parts. The site should be automatically backed up and integrated with Facebook, Twitter, and other social media.

Search engine optimization (SEO) is the process of affecting the visibility of a website in a search engine's unpaid search results. In general, the earlier (or higher ranked on the search results page) and more frequently a site appears in the search results list, the more visitors it will receive from the search engine's users.

This internet marketing strategy considers how search engines work, what people search for, the actual search terms or keywords typed into search engines, and which search engines are preferred by their targeted audience. Optimizing a website may involve editing its content and associated coding to both increase its relevance to specific keywords and remove barriers to the indexing activities of search engines. Promoting a site to increase the number of backlinks, or inbound links, is another tactic.

Often, your website designer is experienced in SEO. Make sure that whomever you choose is ethical. While SEOs can provide clients with valuable services, some unethical SEOs have given the industry a black eye through their overly aggressive marketing efforts and their attempts to manipulate search engine results in unfair ways. Practices that violate search engine guidelines may result in a negative adjustment of your site's presence or even the removal of your site from the index.

Website ads are a way to drive traffic to your website. However, I believe that your money would be better spent on an attractive website and better SEO.

Public Speaking

Everyone has an initial fear of *public speaking*. My first two years in college I sold encyclopedias door-to-door/cold-canvased. That experience eliminated my shyness. If you take my advice and become an officer of organizations in your area of expertise, you'll have many opportunities. Fortunately, in organizations your speaking responsibilities increase gradually from chairman of a committee to four or five years later as president.

Public Speaking Opportunities

Almost any kind of speaking engagement enhances your image and credibility. (See chapter 8 for details.)

Congratulations Notes

Don't miss an opportunity to send a note of congratulations. As your secretary culls through the newspaper (news articles and people in the business news, etc.), FedBizOpps 'FBO' database, and other sources of leads, he or she should be looking for opportunities for you to send a note. An award, a promotion, an appointment, or a selection for a new project are opportunities. Don't just restrict this to people that you know. Have your secretary give the typed note to you for your signature along with the news article. This gives you the opportunity to add something personal, make a phone call, or not send the note at all.

Thank-You Notes

Anytime that someone does something nice for you, send a handwritten note. If you have lunch with a client and he pays, send a note, even though you thanked him at the time. Even if you paid, it doesn't hurt to send him a note thanking him for meeting with you. If a client has you and your wife to dinner at the client's home, bring some fresh flowers in a vase and possibly some good wine. Also, send a thank-you note.

Have a Nice Office

An impressive office will project an image of success and accomplishment. Most clients assume that a successful professional must be an expert in their specialty and will provide exceptional service. Wait until your firm is well-established, then upgrade your office space.

"FREE BONUS"

Starting Your Career – CHECK LIST

and

Your Marketing – TOOL LIST

As a "special gift" for you, I have prepared a **Starting Your Career – CHECK LIST** and a **Your Marketing – TOOL LIST**, both of which you can down load from my website at no cost. The first is a list of the things you shouldn't overlook when starting a professional practice or any kind of business. The second is a concise marketing Tip List - Enjoy!

Go to: https://www.TheEngineersResource.com.

OUTLINE GUIDE

- **Business announcement.** Make your business announcement outstanding. It should look like a wedding invitation on fine, thick paper with raised letters.

- **Letterhead and business cards.** Create elegant letterhead and business cards. Parchment with raised letters and no logo would be a good choice.

- **Brochure.** Your brochure is the face of the company. It will evolve as your firm grows. Try to make it versatile and something that will make you proud and distinguish you from your competitors.

- **Announcements.** Don't forget to send out announcements of awards, new services/specialties, and anniversaries.

- **Your website.** A professional firm's website has become one of the most active sources of new clients. Your website should look professional; hire an experienced professional website designer.

- **Always consider public speaking opportunities**. This is especially important when you're trying to promote a new service or new specialty. Public Speaking Opportunities enhances your image and credibility.

- **Send notes.** Never forget to send thank you notes, and look for opportunities to send notes of congratulations. You don't even need to know someone to recognize their achievements.

- **Open houses and parties.** These are great ways to thank your clients, show off your celebrity clients, and tell all about new specialties and exciting projects.

What people are saying:

Included are more than 100 marketing methods. + I can't believe what great marketing ideas are included. + This book focuses on the top marketing ideas ever used. + These are the best small business tools for any profession. + I ordered two more as gift marketing ideas for my children. + This is one of the best sales and marketing books ever written. + This is a list of sales tools that I can choose from in the future.

CHAPTER 5

YOUR NOTEBOOK AND SUCCESS

INTRODUCTION

Learn why you need to start a notebook to record anything that you might need again. Discover why spending time each week reading about new topics in your field, business trends, and current affairs will enhance your reputation.

Start A Notebook

It's never too early or too late to start building an outstanding reputation. Everyone admires smart people, and it's the most important trait that makes you stand out from your competitors at work and in life.

Once you have a job, do your best to be *exceptional*. Arrive early and leave late. Start a notebook to record information, such as office procedures, your contact list, formulas, calculations, definitions, and anything that you might need again. My notebook was a three-ring binder; yours will be your laptop or iPad.

Ask a lot of questions, but avoid the same question a second time—consult your notebook.

As soon as I started my career as a consulting engineer, I learned that my mentor, John W. King could never answer a question with a yes or a no. His answers always came with a story and a long explanation. This was often frustrating when we were up against a deadline. But it taught me related things, helped me to remember the answers, and gave me an understanding of the why.

Fill Your Notebook with Knowledge

It's critically important that you stay up to date. This involves weekly reading, including magazines in your industry and in your specialty. Also, observe business trends, and keep up-to date with current affairs. This will aid you in your present job and help your future endeavors to thrive and prosper in any economy. Dedicate at least four hours a week to this task. Always have something with you to read. Don't waste time waiting for doctors while reading outdated health care magazines. Every time that you find something interesting, write a white paper. (See chapter 6). Include your conversation Statement." (See chapter 6.)

What Is Success?

The dictionary describes success as "attaining wealth, prosperity and/or fame." However, success means different things to each of us.

In my opinion to be a success in life includes the following components:

- Happiness—for yourself, your loved ones, and those whom you encounter
- Good health—Sufficient to enjoy life and to participate in most activities
- Family and friends—Who you care about and who care for you
- Interests—in both work and leisure activities
- Wealth—sufficient to nicely support yourself and your family
- Respect—from all who know you
- Charity—good deeds for others

When we speak of success, most of us think of job/wealth success, and this is primarily the focus of this book. However, you can't be a true success without most of the components listed here.

Each person needs to define their own meaning of success. I offer these stated components as a starting point. You should expand/edit this list to assist you in reaching your own definition of success. Many of us think that wealth is the starting point; I disagree. I propose that happiness is where to start. Happiness is the key element that will allow you to eventually gain the other components of success. I propose that you embrace the concept of personal success in lieu of job/wealth success. Although the right job and personal wealth should not be overlooked.

What Does Success Mean to You?

Don't just think about success. Take the time to actually write down your own ideas of the components of success and then prioritize them in the order of importance to you. Don't just make a list that you think others will find praiseworthy. Realize that success is a multifaceted personal concept. Assume that you're the only one who will ever see these thoughts. Include your innermost feelings. Print out your list and carry it with you for the next week. Look at it at least three times a day and modify it as thoughts occur to you. Refer to your success list when making all important decisions in your life and modify your list as you mature, grow and learn life's lessons.

OUTLINE GUIDE

- **Your notebook:** to record information, such as office procedures, your contact list, formulas, calculations, definitions, and anything that you might need again

- **Spend time:** reading magazines in your industry, plus articles regarding business trends, and current affairs

- **Success:** includes happiness, good health, family and friends, interests, wealth, respect, and charity.

- **Starting point:** happiness and not wealth. But wealth should not be overlooked.

- **Make a prioritized list:** of your own ideas of the components of success.

What people are saying:

Included are more than 100 marketing methods. + I can't believe what great marketing ideas are included. + This book focuses on the top marketing ideas ever used. + These are the best small business tools for any profession. + I ordered two more as gift marketing ideas for my children. + This is one of the best sales and marketing books ever written. + This is a list of sales tools that I can choose from in the future.

CHAPTER 6

WHITE PAPERS

INTRODUCTION

Learn what a white paper is and how it will be useful in promoting your reputation as the smartest person in the room. Understand the need to commit much of the information to memory. Glean how white papers can possibly be the basis of a magazine article authored by you. Ascertain why writing papers on new topics may lead to new services for you. Gain knowledge of the steps for writing and organizing your white papers. Realize that, if you serve as an expert witness, white papers will help you to prepare for your report, deposition, testimony and cross-examination.

Prepare White Papers

A white paper is a report or guide to help readers to understand an issue. When your work involves a new technical issue, read about it and take detailed notes in narrative form, including definitions of the various new terms.

Organize your notes and add this white paper to your notebook. Start as soon as you have a job. After you have prepared a white paper, reread it several times, and commit much of the information to memory. When the subject comes up, you'll be able to discuss it like an expert and before long everyone will consider you the smartest person in the room. White papers will serve as a useful future reference and possibly the basis of a magazine article authored by you.

As an electrical consulting engineer, I primarily designed electrical systems for buildings, and I soon developed white papers on the following subjects:

- illumination (lighting)
- clock and program systems
- sound reinforcement systems
- intercom systems
- door intercom systems
- private telephone system
- media retrieval systems
- burglar alarm or vandal alarms
- card access systems
- TV (master antenna, closed circuit, cable)
- video surveillance systems
- emergency battery lighting
- emergency/stand-by generators
- dimming systems
- fire alarm systems
- fire detection systems
- nurse call systems
- lightning protection
- building structural grounding
- snow melting (roof, walks, driveways)
- computer rooms
- UPS systems (uninterruptible power supplies)
- harmonic provisions
- power monitors
- TVSS and surge protectors
- theatrical lighting

Depending on your career choice, your white papers will be on very different topics. But it's important that they cover the topics that you're expected to know and understand.

From time to time, new topics will come up in your industry. Be the first to investigate these, write a white paper, and be the expert on this new topic.

At various times in my career as an electrical consulting engineer, I investigated new topics of the day, wrote a white paper on the topic, and as a result, offered the following new services:

Electromagnetic Field Investigations and Mitigation

Several years ago, EMFs (electromagnetic fields) were a hot topic. Many people became concerned that the electromagnetic fields emitted by low-frequency (sixty cycle) power sources might cause serious health concerns. People were especially apprehensive about their proximity to high voltage power lines. Some people changed to wind-up alarm clocks rather than sleep with a small electric motor near their heads.

I bought a couple of gauss meters, took measurements, and did some studying. Then I wrote a white paper, followed by an article that was published in a national magazine. I identified and quantified the sources; I left the health issues to others. I became a member of the National Electromagnetic Field Testing Association. Later, I was a guest speaker at the National Conference on Harmonics and Power Quality in Philadelphia, Pennsylvania. I was the go-to guy for magnetic field projects. In office buildings and in universities, computer screens were distorted due to proximity to power sources. In data centers, computers were acting erratically for the same reason. My services would start with a study, including measuring and mapping the fields, recommending solutions, and estimating costs of mitigation. This was often followed by a design phase, bid phase, and construction observation phase. I didn't have any competition, and I was well paid for both my services and expertise.

Power Quality Services

Another hot topic was power quality. Basically, on a three-phase power system, each of the phases are separated 120 degrees from each other, which causes cancelation and results in very little neutral current. However, for computer loads, a third harmonic current can occur, causing the neutral current to exceed the phase currents. I did some studying, took measurements, wrote a white paper and some articles and again, was considered an expert, and did quite a few power quality studies, and most included preparation of one-line diagrams on an hourly basis. Again, no competition, well paid.

Uninterruptable Power Systems (UPS)

A UPS is a device consisting of a battery and an inverter to provide AC power to a load without interruption if commercial power fails. You can buy a small UPS at your local electronics store. You don't need an engineer to design the installation. Just plug your computer into it, and no information is lost during a blackout.

However, systems for computer rooms are huge and complex and require engineering, including paralleling of units, backup generators, bypass for uninterrupted maintenance, and complicated cooling. After a large installation, I wrote a white paper followed by a magazine article titled, "UPS Installation at Bank Data Center is expandable to 5 Megawatts." I was then considered the data center/UPS expert.

A few years later, a US manufacturer of small UPS units bought a Danish company that manufactured large units. They had the technical manuals and catalogs converted to English, but they were concerned because the result was what they called "Danglish." I wasn't sure what they wanted from me, but when they called, I went to meet with them. Two young guys met me in the reception area and took me to the cafeteria to discuss it over coffee. While I was giving my usual "spiel" to the thirty-year-old manager, his twenty-five-year-old assistant was thumbing through my brochure. First, the assistant interrupted to say, "There is an article here that he wrote about 'power quality.'" Next, he said, "He also wrote an article about a UPS system that he designed."

At this point, the manager held up his hand to stop me from talking and said, "We have done a nationwide search, and yours is the only name that has come up more than once. We don't know what you're going to charge, but you're the guy we want."

This was a very unusual assignment; it was not an engineering design. I gave them two proposals:

The first proposal was to rewrite the text of the catalog, rewrite the white papers, and explain how to reorganize the catalog to be more user friendly for consulting engineers. I was also specific on the number of review meetings.

The second proposal (which they hadn't asked for) was for me to be available for telephone consultations for up to eight hours per month for a monthly fee. This was a whole new area of business for them, and they were not used to marketing their product to consulting engineers and to data center managers. I didn't work for cheap, but I restrained myself from overcharging.

They accepted both proposals. After three months with no telephone consultations, I started to spend a few hours each month reviewing catalog material of their competitors and industry magazines. I sent them emails with suggestions for new related products and services. They were happy with the catalog work and continued my monthly fee for over a year, without ever calling me for a consultation. They also became a client for numerous UPS and data center designs as well as some upgrades at their various manufacturing facilities.

Arc Flash Calculations

More recently, another hot topic called arc flash became a concern. Since the days of Thomas Edison, the largest electrical concern has been short-circuits: the high inrush of current when two opposite polarity electrical wires touch. A newer concern is arc flash: the heat and flash associated with the same event. (Google "arc flash" for some gruesome videos.)

I, again, became considered an expert and did many arc-flash studies, and most included preparation of one-line diagrams, fault-current calculations, and panel labeling on an hourly basis. Again, no competition (at the time), and well paid.

Look around for an opportunity to become an expert on a current topic and the chance to offer a new service with little competition and unrestrained fees.

How to Write a White Paper

- Search for information
- Highlight relevant data
- Compile your paper in the following way:
  - Introduction/summary (conversationally)
  - Why the topic is important
  - Details
  - Close

White Paper Examples

The following is an interesting article that I found on-line regarding a new concept in AI (artificial intelligence) called RL (reinforced learning). By experimenting, computers are figuring out how to do things that no programmer could teach them. Note: I have added highlighting.

Original Article Used to Create a White Paper

Reinforcement Learning

By experimenting, computers are figuring out how to do things that no programmer could teach them.

Availability: 1 to 2 years

MIT Technology Review

• by Will Knight

Inside a simple computer simulation, a group of self-driving cars are performing a crazy-looking maneuver on a four-lane virtual highway. Half are trying to move from the right-hand lanes just as the other half try to merge from the left. It seems like just the sort of tricky thing that might flummox a robot vehicle, but they manage it with precision.

I'm watching the driving simulation at the biggest artificial-intelligence conference of the year, held in Barcelona this past December. What's most amazing is that the software governing the cars' behavior wasn't programmed in the conventional sense at all. It learned how to merge, slickly and safely, simply by practicing. During training, the control software performed the maneuver over and over, altering its instructions a little with each attempt. Most of the time the merging happened way too slowly and cars interfered with each other. But whenever the merge went smoothly, the system would learn to favor the behavior that led up to it.

This approach, known as reinforcement learning, is largely how AlphaGo, a computer developed by a subsidiary of Alphabet called DeepMind, mastered the impossibly complex board game Go and beat one of the best human players in the world in a high-profile match last year. Now reinforcement learning may soon inject greater intelligence into much more than games. In addition to improving self-driving cars, the technology can get a robot to grasp objects it has never seen before, and it can figure out the optimal configuration for the equipment in a data center.

Reinforcement learning copies a very simple principle from nature. The psychologist Edward Thorndike documented it more than 100 years ago. Thorndike placed cats inside boxes from which they could escape only by pressing a lever. After a considerable amount of pacing around and meowing, the animals would eventually step on the lever by chance. After they learned to associate this behavior with the desired outcome, they eventually escaped with increasing speed.

Some of the very earliest artificial-intelligence researchers believed that this process might be usefully reproduced in machines. In 1951, Marvin Minsky, a student at Harvard who would become one of the founding fathers of AI as a professor at MIT, built a machine that used a simple form of reinforcement learning to mimic a rat learning to navigate a maze. Minsky's Stochastic Neural Analogy Reinforcement Computer, or SNARC, consisted of dozens of tubes, motors, and clutches that simulated the behavior of 40 neurons and synapses. As a simulated rat made its way out of a virtual maze, the strength of some synaptic connections would increase, thereby reinforcing the underlying behavior.

There were few successes over the next few decades. In 1992, Gerald Tesauro, a researcher at IBM, demonstrated a program that used the technique to play backgammon. It became skilled enough to rival the best human players, a landmark achievement in AI. But reinforcement learning proved difficult to scale to more complex problems. "People thought it was a cool idea that didn't really work," says David Silver, a researcher at DeepMind in the U.K. and a leading proponent of reinforcement learning today.

That view changed dramatically in March 2016, however. That's when AlphaGo, a program trained using reinforcement learning, destroyed one of the best Go players of all time, South Korea's Lee Sedol. The feat was astonishing, because it's virtually impossible to build a good Go-playing program with conventional programming. Not only is the game extremely complex, but even accomplished Go players may struggle to say why certain moves are good or bad, so the principles of the game are difficult to write into code. Most AI researchers had expected that it would take a decade for a computer to play the game as well as an expert human.

Reinforcement Learning

- Breakthrough: An approach to artificial intelligence that gets computers to learn like people, without explicit instruction.

- Why It Matters: Progress in self-¬driving cars and other forms of automation will slow dramatically unless machines can hone skills through experience.

- Key Players
  - DeepMind
  - Mobileye
  - Open AI
  - Google
  - Uber

- Availability1 to 2 years

Jostling for position

Silver, a mild-mannered Brit who became fascinated with artificial intelligence as an undergraduate at the University of Cambridge, explains why reinforcement learning has recently become so formidable. He says that the key is combining it with deep learning, a technique that involves using a very large simulated neural network to recognize patterns in data (see "10 Breakthrough Technologies 2013: Deep Learning").

Reinforcement learning works because researchers figured out how to get a computer to calculate the value that should be assigned to, say, each right or wrong turn that a rat might make on its way out of its maze. Each value is stored in a large table, and the computer updates all these values as it learns. For large and complicated tasks, this becomes computationally impractical. In recent years, however, deep learning has proved an extremely efficient way to recognize patterns in data, whether the data refers to the turns in a maze, the positions on a Go board, or the pixels shown on screen during a computer game.

In fact, it was in games that DeepMind made its name. In 2013 it published details of a program capable of learning to play various Atari video games at a superhuman level, leading Google to acquire the company for more than $500 million in 2014. These and other feats have in turn inspired other researchers and companies to turn to reinforcement learning. A number of industrial-robot makers are testing the approach as a way to train their machines to perform new tasks without manual programming. And researchers at Google, also an Alphabet subsidiary, worked with DeepMind to use deep reinforcement learning to make its data centers more energy efficient. It's difficult to figure out how all the elements in a data center will affect energy usage, but a reinforcement-learning algorithm can learn from collated data and experiment in simulation to suggest, say, how and when to operate the cooling systems.

The setting where you'll probably most notice this software's remarkably humanlike behavior is in self-driving cars. Today's driverless vehicles often falter in complex situations that involve interacting with human drivers, such as traffic circles or four-way stops. If we don't want them to take unnecessary risks, or to clog the roads by being overly hesitant, they will need to acquire more nuanced driving skills, like jostling for position in a crowd of other cars.

The highway merging software was demoed in Barcelona by Mobileye, an Israeli automotive company that makes vehicle safety systems used by dozens of carmakers, including Tesla Motors (see "50 Smartest Companies 2016"). After screening the merging clip, Shai Shalev-Shwartz, Mobileye's vice president for technology, shows some of the challenges self-driving cars will face: a bustling roundabout in Jerusalem; a frenetic intersection in Paris; and a hellishly chaotic scene from a road in India. "If a self-driving car follows the law precisely, then during rush hour I might wait in a merge situation for an hour," Shalev-Shwartz says.

Mobileye plans to test the software on a fleet of vehicles in collaboration with BMW and Intel later this year. Both Google and Uber say they are also testing reinforcement learning for their self-driving vehicles.

Reinforcement learning led to AlphaGo's stunning victory over a human Go champion last year.

Reinforcement learning is being applied in a growing number of areas, says Emma Brunskill, an assistant professor at Stanford University who specializes in the approach. But she says it's well suited to automated driving because it enables "good sequences of decisions." Progress would proceed much more slowly if programmers had to encode all such decisions into cars in advance.

But there are challenges to overcome, too. Andrew Ng, chief scientist at the Chinese company Baidu, warns that the approach requires a huge amount of data, and that many of its successes have come when a computer could practice relentlessly in simulations. Indeed, researchers are still figuring out just how to make reinforcement learning work in complex situations in which there is more than one objective. Mobileye has had to tweak its protocols so a self-driving car that is adept at avoiding accidents won't be more likely to cause one for someone else.

When you watch the outlandish merging demo, it looks as though the company has succeeded, at least so far. But later this year, perhaps on a highway near you, reinforcement learning will get its most dramatic and important tests to date.

Note that I have highlighted what I felt were the most interesting and relevant parts of the article. The following is the white paper that I created from the article:

White Paper Created from Online Article

Reinforcement Learning

I recently read a few articles regarding a new concept in AI (artificial intelligence) called RL (reinforced learning). By experimenting, computers are figuring out how to do things that no programmer could teach them. It's expected to be perfected in one to two years.

You'll probably most notice this software's remarkably humanlike behavior in self-driving cars. Today's driverless vehicles often falter in complex situations that involve interacting with human drivers, such as traffic circles or four-way stops. If we don't want them to take unnecessary risks, or to clog the roads by being overly hesitant, they will need to acquire more nuanced driving skills, like jostling for position in a crowd of other cars.

What's most amazing, using "reinforced learning," is that the software governing the cars' behavior wasn't programmed in the conventional sense at all. It learned how to merge, slickly and safely, simply by practicing. During training, the control software performed the maneuver over and over, altering its instructions a little with each attempt. Most of the time the merging happened way too slowly and cars interfered with each other. But whenever the merge went smoothly, the system would learn to favor the behavior that led up to it. Some say that "if a self-driving car follows the law precisely, then during rush hours It might wait in a merge situation for an hour." So, in addition to speeding up the process, engineers are tweaking protocols so a self-driving car that is adept at avoiding accidents won't be more likely to cause one for someone else.

In addition to improving self-driving cars, the technology can get a robot to grasp objects, that it has never seen before, and it can figure out the optimal configuration for the equipment in a data center.

Configuration of White Paper Suitable for Reuse in Article Authored by You

Reinforcement Learning

I recently read a few articles regarding a new concept in AI (artificial intelligence) called RL (reinforced learning). By experimenting, computers are figuring out how to do things that no programmer could teach them. It's expected to be perfected in one to two years.

You'll probably most notice this software's amazingly humanlike behavior in self-driving vehicles. Today's driverless automobiles often waver in convoluted circumstances like relating with human drivers at complex intersections. If we don't want them to take unnecessary risks, or to clog the roads by being too cautious, they will need to acquire more nuanced driving talents, like maneuvering for position in a crowd of other vehicles.

What's most astonishing about "reinforced learning" is that the software governing the cars' behavior wasn't programmed in the normal way. The software learned how to merge, slickly and safely, merely by attempting. The control software performed the maneuver over and over, varying its commands a little with each effort. Most of the time, the blending occurred too sluggishly, and cars interfered with each other. But whenever the combining went smoothly, the system would learn to favor the actions that led up to it. Some say that "if a self-driving car follows the law too exactly, it might wait in a merge situation for an hour or longer." So, in addition to speeding up the process, engineers are tweaking protocols so a self-driving car will be adept at avoiding accidents and won't be likely to cause one for someone else.

In addition to perfecting self-driving cars, reinforcement learning can allow robots to grasp objects that they have never encountered before, lay out the most favorable configuration for the equipment in a data center, and teach computers to beat humans at complex games.

Expert Witnesses Use White Papers

In the latter part of my career as a consulting electrical engineer, I often did forensic engineering; investigating electrocutions, fires of electrical origin, and electrical equipment failures. This including consulting to attorneys and serving as an expert witness in courts of law.

To properly prepare a case, it's often necessary to research specialized areas of your field, such as those that may be new to you or that you haven't needed since college. While doing this studying, make notes in a narrative form to make it easier for you to later write your expert report. In addition, these notes will help you to prepare for your deposition, testimony, and cross-examination regarding the specialized technical area at issue. They have the added advantage of preparing you for questions in the general technical area but not necessarily specific to the case at hand.

OUTLINE GUIDE

- **White paper**: A white paper is a report or guide to help readers to understand an issue.

- **Memorize:** After you have prepared a white paper, reread it several times, and commit much of the information to memory.

- **Other uses:** White papers will serve as a useful future reference and possibly the basis of a magazine article authored by you.

- **New topics:** Investigate new topics of the day in your industry, write a white paper, and offer new services regarding the subject matter.

- **How to write a white paper:**
  - search for information
  - highlight relevant data
  - introduction/summary (conversationally.)
  - why the topic is important
  - details
  - close

- **Expert witness:** If you serve as an expert witness, white papers will help you to prepare for your report, deposition, testimony, and cross-examination.

What people are saying:

Included are more than 100 marketing methods. + I can't believe what great marketing ideas are included. + This book focuses on the top marketing ideas ever used. + These are the best small business tools for any profession. + I ordered two more as gift marketing ideas for my children. + This is one of the best sales and marketing books ever written. + This is a list of sales tools that I can choose from in the future.

CHAPTER 7

CONVERSATION QUESTIONS
AND STATEMENTS

INTRODUCTION

Realize that people judge your intelligence when you first meet. Learn how to let the circumstances of meeting someone determine the start of the conversation. Understand why you should encourage the other person to speak. Discover what a *conversation statement* is and why you need one. Topics that you might include: about me, books, movies, concerts, travel, and hobbies. Notice why you should commit most of your *conversation statement* to memory. Grasp why asking about the person that you're meeting is a priority.

Starting a Conversation

When meeting someone for the first time, starting a conversation can often be awkward and uncomfortable. I recommend letting the circumstances of the meeting determine the start. If you meet at a personal event, like a house party or wedding, say, "Hi, I'm _____. I work with Gary. How do you know Gary and Alice?" If you meet in a public place, perhaps say, "Hi, I'm _____. I haven't seen you hear before. Do you come hear often?

Notice that these conversation starters have two parts: first, an introduction, and second, a question. The introduction alerts the person that you're talking to them, and the question prompts a response. Be prepared with follow-up questions like: Are you from this area?

That reminds me of a joke: A woman went into her favorite bar in Florida. After a while, a handsome man came in and sat next to her. She said, "I haven't seen you here before. Is this your first visit?"

He responded, "Actually, this is my first time back in twenty years."

She asked, "Why so long?"

He replied, "I've been in prison."

She inquired, "Why?"

He replied, "I'm not proud of it, but I killed my wife."

She said with a smile, "Oh, so you're single!"

Conversation Questions

Conversations should include both questions and statements. But encourage the other person to speak. People like to talk about themselves and their interests. Surprisingly, if the other person speaks two-thirds of the time, they will rate *you* as a great conversationalist.

It's usually best to precede questions with statements: "I am an electrical engineer, and I designed electrical systems for buildings—lighting, power, fire alarm systems, for example. What type of work do you do?"

Conversation Statement

Make a list of things about you that you may want to share with others and questions that you could ask to learn about people that you meet and to show an interest in them.

We all have this list in our heads, but we can't always think of each category or the names and details on the spur of the moment. Study and memorize your list and start to be considered the smartest person in the room.

About Me

Your family, career, where you live, and interests.

Books

Three favorite authors and books; and be prepared to voice three-to-six sentences about each book.

Movies

Three favorite movies and be ready to speak three-to-six sentences about each.

Concerts

Your three favorite entertainers

Travel

Information about your trips to interesting places, both past and planned.

Hobbies

How you spend your spare time.

Conversations (Page 1 of 2)

My Conversation Statement

About Me

Met my wife, Pat, at her best friend's sixteenth birthday party. I was seventeen, and she was fifteen. We dated for seven years and were married for forty-one years. She died six months before I retired. But I am blessed; we were together almost fifty years.

We have two children and two grandchildren.

I am an EE. I started my own consulting engineering firm on my twenty-ninth birthday. I later added forensic engineering, and we grew to eleven people. I sold to a large engineering firm, and retired.

I split my time between my homes in Rhode Island and Florida. I play pool, read, and write and publish books.

Books

Michael Connelly
   Harry Bosch—Los Angeles

John Sanford
   Lucas Davenport—The Prey series—Minnesota

James Patterson—many books

Movies

Fury—Brad Pitt, WWII Tank movie

Braveheart—Mel Gibson—Gibson portrays William Wallace, a thirteenth-century Scottish warrior who led the Scots in the First War of Scottish Independence.

Star Wars—The first film in the series, *Star Wars*, was released in 1977. It was one of the first movies to mix animation with human characters.

Concerts

Neil Diamond—Fenway Park—It has been twenty-three years since I had a "hit." Yet here I am, and there you are.

Billy Joel

Elton John

Conversations (Page 2 of 2)

Travel

Hawaii—This summer, I took both my grandchildren to Hawaii. We stayed in a hotel for three days and toured Honolulu. We then took a seven-day Norwegian cruise that visited five other islands, and on the way home, we spent two days in Los Angeles.

San Francisco—Last summer, I took both of my grandchildren to San Francisco. We spent two nights at Yosemite National Park followed by five nights in the city.

Europe—France and Italy with fifteen-year-old grandson; later, the same trip with my four-teen- year-old granddaughter.

Three nights in **Paris** (St. Germain), no French food—not even a croissant—pizza or McDonald's, Moulin Rouge (His first taste of champagne and possibly his first view of live titties.), Catacombs, Botobus de Paris, and Monet's gardens at Giverny.

We traveled by train to other cities:

Carcassonne, France—a thirteenth-century walled city; Monte Carlo, Monaco; Nice, France; Sirmione, Italy—a castle on Lake Gouda with harbor for the lake fleet; Verona, Italy—the home of Romeo and Juliet; Venice, Italy—gondolas, St. Mark's Square, Palazzo Ducale, Murano; Sorento, Italy; Amalfi, Italy; Rome, Italy.

Ireland (Ring of Kerry) and **England** (London)

Baltic Cruise (Chorley in Lancashire)

South America—Norwegian Cruise including Panama Cannel

Bermuda The Reefs Hotel; great weather any time of year.

Caribbean including Nassau and Paradise Island

Home Exchanges (Norborne-Grison, France; Verona, Italy; Vancouver, Canada; Seattle, WA; Acapulco, Mexico.)

US National Parks (including Chicago, Illinois; Las Vegas and Los Angeles including Michael Connelly's—Harry Bosch's places.

Hobbies

Pool (packet billiards); reading; gym; writing and publishing books.

After you prepare your conversation statement, try to commit most of it to memory. If you keep referring to your notes, you'll not look smart.

Do not tell your whole life story before asking about the person you're meeting. After talking about basics, here are some suggestions:

- "Since I've been retired, I've found the time to read. My favorite author is Michael Connelly. He has written twenty-four detective novels based in Los Angeles with the main character, Harry Bosch. The key reason that I like these books so much is that Harry is brilliant, but abrasive. Do you do much reading?"
- If they say no, move on to another topic: "What do you like to do in your spare time?" or "Tell me a little bit more about yourself." Give a nice smile and wait for a response before proceeding.
- "What is your favorite movie? Or "Have you seen any good movies lately?"
- "I love live concerts. My favorite performers are Neil Diamond, Billy Joel, and Elton John. I once attended a concert with both Billy Joel and Elton John at the Boston Garden. It was great! Have you been to any live concerts?"
- "Last summer I took both of my grandchildren to San Francisco. Their two favorite things were the view of downtown from Alamo Park and having a "Worst Shirt" contest in the vintage clothing stores at Hate Asbury. On the way home, both grandchildren said that San Francisco is their favorite city. Have you done much traveling?"
- "Since I have been retired, my hobby has been writing and publishing books. It's a lot of fun and it keeps me busy. What hobbies do you have?"

But remember that most people like to talk about themselves and their interests. So encourage them to talk. Try to look interested and ask lots of questions.

If you can't get meaningful responses, move on. There are usually some interesting people in every group.

OUTLINE GUIDE

- **Starting a conversation:** Let the circumstances of the meeting determine the start of the conversation.

- **Encourage the other person to speak:** If the other person speaks two-thirds of the time, they will rate *you* as a great conversationalist.

- **Prepare a conversation statement:** Make a list of things about you and questions that you might ask.

- **Topics that you might include:** About me, books, movies, concerts, travel and hobbies.

- **Memorize:** Try to commit most of your conversation statement to memory. If you keep referring to your notes, you'll not look smart.

- **Priority:** Asking about the person that you're meeting is paramount.

What people are saying:

Included are more than 100 marketing methods. + I can't believe what great marketing ideas are included. + This book focuses on the top marketing ideas ever used. + These are the best small business tools for any profession. + I ordered two more as gift marketing ideas for my children. + This is one of the best sales and marketing books ever written. + This is a list of sales tools that I can choose from in the future.

PUBLICATIONS AND PROMOTION

INTRODUCTION

Understand why collecting business cards and starting a contact list will help your reputation. Realize why you should expand your mailing list to include all the players in your industry. Find out how many mailings to send and what kind of things to include. Ascertain how to select topics for your articles and how to submit them to magazines. Learn how to design, print and distribute re-prints of your articles. Finally see why almost any kind of speaking engagement enhances your image and credibility.

Contact List

In chapter 3, we discussed collecting business cards from those that you want to get to know and starting a contact list, including both business and personal information.

I recommend using a contact form for each person on your list. At the top of each sheet would be the same information as on a mailing label, plus telephone and fax numbers as well as email address. Also, note company affiliation and any personal information, including how you met (if you have) or how you know of them.

The purpose of these contact forms is so you'll remember when and how the person got on your mailing list. They may have called you for a fee proposal, you may have met them at a meeting, or you may have found their name online. Each time that you contact the person, list the date and details on this sheet. You may find a computer program to do all of this for you; the important thing is to have this information in some easily accessible form.

Mailing List

When I first started my electrical consulting engineering practice, all my clients were architects, and there were about thirty potential clients listed in the phonebook's Yellow Pages. But by the end of my first year, my mailing list had expanded to over five hundred names. I included all the architects (even those who I didn't know or said they used someone else). Each time that I prepared a fee proposal for someone not on the list, I added them. In addition, I added the following:

- electrical inspectors (People inquire: Who should I get to draw my electrical plans?)
- electrical supply companies (Same question.)
- electrical contractors (Same question, plus they may hire your firm for design–build projects.)
- housing authorities (Director and facilities manager.)
- superintendents of fire alarms (People inquire: Who do I hire to design my fire alarm system?)
- power company representatives (Plus, president and department heads.)
- electrical manufacturers' representatives (Many also call on architects.)
- hospitals (Director of facilities and president.)
- universities (Director of facilities and president.)

Make your own list to suit your clients and industry. Your first mailing should be your business announcement.

Once you're in business, I recommend a minimum of two mailings per year.

I used to send Thanksgivings cards; people notice them because they don't get many, and it avoids a religious connotation associated with Christmas.

Newsletters

My second mailing was often what I titled as an "update." These are now more commonly referred to as *newsletters*. It was always a single page (multiple pages don't get read), printed on my letterhead, and placed unfolded (easily filed) in a 9x12 envelope (it looks more important in a large envelope). I included mention of exciting projects, employee promotions, new services being offered, and so on. Sometimes, my second mailing was a reprint of a magazine article about my projects or about a timely technical issue authored by me. See "Articles" later in this chapter.

Send all mailings to your entire mailing list, even if the contact may not be interested or may not be a potential client. They will remember you as an expert and recommend you.

I have had people question the value of an expanded mailing list, and I offer the following story:

I had a new client consisting of two partners. One wanted a variance (exception from a code requirement) regarding exit signs. The other said, "Don't waste your time. I applied for a variance three times on a previous project in that city, and they turned me down on all three." The client decided to apply anyway. So he did the paperwork and listed me as the electrical engineer. I had to go to the hearing with him (for free) to present our case.

At these hearings, cases are usually heard on a first-come, first-served basis; unfortunately, my client was at the last minute. As we entered the rear of the hearing room, the variance committee chairman (whom I didn't know) was standing at the front and saw us enter. He said in a loud voice, "Welcome, Mr. Gaskell. We have a seat down here in the front for you. You can go first, and whatever you want, you get."

As it turned out, the chairman was a small (politically connected) electrical contractor whom I had never met but who was on my mailing list and recognized me from my picture, which I included on many of my mailings. I'm not saying that this moment of recognition made my self-promotion all worthwhile, but it impressed this client and eventually gained me a nationwide reputation.

Follow this formula for promoting yourself, and your firm will become well known and you'll soon be considered the smartest person in the room.

Articles

During my second or third year in business, power companies started to reduce their voltage to conserve energy. Clients became concerned that this might have a deleterious effect on their motors, lights, and electrical systems. I did some reading of textbooks and handbooks (Of course there was no internet in my early career.), made some calculations to quantify the results, and included this information in an update newsletter. It got rave reviews, so I expanded this information into a magazine article that, to my surprise, got published.

I ordered one thousand reprints from the magazine and sent some of them to my mailing list. I used the extras as filler to my brochure. Overnight, I was thought to be an expert and the smartest person in the room.

If you get published, you too can gain a reputation as an expert. I recommend the following:

- Select the most popular magazine in your industry, the one that everyone in your industry reads.
- Review your project list, and select your most interesting recent project. Those that are appealing to magazine editors are prominent or use methods, materials, or techniques that are new or unusual.
- Alternatively, write about a timely issue in your industry. But first read the last twelve issues of the magazine to be sure that this topic has not already been exhaustively reviewed. If you can relate the topic to one or more of your projects, your chances of publication are improved.
- If your article mentions a project, you must verify that your client and the building owner/developer won't object to the mention of their project. An email response is a good thing to have in your records. One of my published articles was about an interesting generator upgrade at a local federal government facility. I later included a reprint when applying for another project at the same facility. I received a cease-and-desist letter from the contracting officer, and despite my profuse apology, I didn't get another project at that facility for a couple of years. Most clients are delighted, but don't skip this step and don't wait until after you have spent a lot of time writing the article.
- Study previous articles and format your article to match the magazine.
- Include many pictures with captions; you should be in some of them.
- Include a headshot photo of yourself.
- Include a brief biography (the same length as normally used in the magazine).
- Include sketches and one-line diagrams if appropriate.
- Call the magazine editor. Introduce yourself, and tell him a little about yourself and your submission. Ask to whom you should address the submission, and obtain both the email address and the mailing address.
- Don't submit the same article to another publication unless you receive a rejection, but don't get discouraged. This is still a great promotional

idea, even if the circulation of the magazine that accepts your article is smaller than your neighborhood; reprints are the key.

Reprints of Articles

I recommend the following regarding reprints:

Contact the publication. They usually have a third party who handles reprints.

Design your reprint:

- If possible, it should all be "one-piece" (single fold—four printable surfaces, or two-fold—6 printable surfaces).
- The first page should be the magazine cover of the issue (delete extraneous items and the date to avoid limiting future use).
- The following pages are your article (delete advertisements and extraneous items).
- The last page should be your company description, including your credentials and a picture of you.
- If you have an extra page, make the blank page your last, but print your company name, address, and so on at the bottom. If the article introduces a new company service, reprint the announcement here.
- Use glossy paper.
- Print in black-and-white; color is too expensive.
- Print enough copies for your initial mailing plus stuffers for your brochure.

The following are several examples:

- Article about one of our projects, "Upgradable Power Conditioning Unit Serves Law Firm," by the senior editor of *Electrical Construction and Maintenance* (*EC&M*) magazine. It was 11x17 and folded in half. I added our company name to the front cover and deleted distracting information. Also, I deleted the publication date to extend the usage of these reprints.

- Article about one of our projects and technical information on the problem that we solved, "Power Factor Improvement Provides Multiple Benefits," by the senior editor of *EC&M*. It was two pieces: 11x17 outer folded cover with an 8½x11 insert.

- Article about a technical issue, "Electrical Design with EMF in Mind," written by me and published in *EC&M*. It was 11x17 folded sheet. See Figure 8-1.

- Article about one of our projects and technical information on the problem that we solved, "Expandable UPS Serves Bank Operations Center," written by me and published in *EC&M*. It was two 11x17 sheets folded and stapled on the fold. I finally got smart and added information to the back cover: me, my firm, and the technical issue addressed in my article.

- Article about a problem that I solved, "Anatomy of a Power Outage," written by me and published in *EC&M*. It was an 11x17 folded sheet.

- Article about a technical issue, "Avoiding EMFs—Designing Buildings Limiting Occupants Exposure to EMFs," written by me and published in *EC&M*. It was two pieces: 11x17 outer folded cover with an 8½x11 insert. I added my resume on the last page. It was this article that gained me the notoriety that resulted in my being invited to speak at the National Conference on Harmonics and Power Quality in Philadelphia, Pennsylvania.

ELECTRICAL CONSTRUCTION AND MAINTENANCE

Electrical Design With EMF In Mind

What are electromagnetic fields and what efforts should be made to minimize them in designing electrical systems today?

ELECTRICAL ENGINEERING BY GASKELL ASSOCIATES, LTD. CONSULTING ENGINEERS

FIGURE 8-1 (1 OF 3)

WHAT'S THE STORY

Electrical Design With EMF In Mind

What are electromagnetic fields and what efforts should be made to minimize them in designing electrical systems today?

John D. Gaskell, P.E.
John D. Gaskell, P.E. is President of Gaskell Associates, Ltd., a consulting engineering firm in Warwick, R.I., and a member of the National Electromagnetic Field Testing Association.

A magnetic field meter assembly consists of a digital multimeter, modified for additional shielding, and a magnetic sensor.

While it may be years before a clear consensus is established on the health risks of electromagnetic fields (EMF) exposure, the topic remains highly controversial. In the meantime, electrical systems can be designed and installed to minimize the extent of the magnetic field component of EMF, often at little or no added cost. Before discussing the steps that can be taken during the design stages of electrical distribution systems, let's find out what EMF is.

What is EMF?

EMF at 60Hz is really made up of two separate entities: electric fields and magnetic fields. An *electric* field, which exists when voltage is present and which is easily blocked by metal, can cause currents to flow on the *surface* of the human body. Electric fields are *not* generally considered to be a biological hazard.

A *magnetic* field, which exists when current flows and which is *not* appreciably blocked by common materials, can cause current to flow *through* the human body. Magnetic fields at 60 Hz *are* considered a possible biological hazard.

A magnetic field decreases as the distance from the source increases. However, the configuration of the source actually determines how quickly a field diminishes. Multiple conductors with current flowing in opposite directions or 3-phase circuits have magnetic fields that are inversely proportional to the distance *squared*. Appliances and transformers are point sources and their fields drops off inversely proportional to the distance *cubed*.

Exposure factors

Without consensus in the scientific community that a hazard actually exists, economics play a big factor in setting limits. We don't know for sure whether long-term, low-level exposure is worse than short-term, high-level exposure.

Some say that switched fields are more dangerous than steady-state fields. Individual characteristics of the person being exposed may need to be considered; age, health, and even fertility and pregnancy may be factors. Obviously, more research is needed. But in the meantime, it may be practical to make some educated guesses, set some *interim* exposure limits, and consider some changes in design.

Practical design suggestions

Services. For an overhead MV service lateral, consider selecting spacer cable in lieu of cross-arm construction. Utilities are becoming more sensitive to the magnetic field issue and may welcome your suggestions. Another choice for a service lateral, of course, is an underground service.

Preferably, pass a service lateral under a storage room rather than an office that is occupied for long time periods. If this cannot be done, then the service lateral should be enclosed in a metallic raceway. The magnetic field will induce a counter EMF in the metallic raceway, which will help reduce the field.

Locate pad-mounted transformers at least 20 ft from buildings. Another consideration is to encircle a pad-mounted transformer with a fence, located at a 4- to 6-ft distance from the edge of the pad.

Switchboards and panels. Locate distribution equipment on exterior walls or walls adjacent to storage areas or corridors. Where possible, locate free-standing switchboards to allow 3 ft of working space on all sides. Use walls abutting occupied spaces for telephone or fire alarm equipment. Avoid locating an electrical room directly below or above an occupied space.

Indoor transformers. Although a typical dry-type, step-down power transformer creates a large magnetic field, this field's strength dissipates very quickly. However, it would still be good practice to locate such a unit in an electrical room remote from occupied spaces.

Bus duct. For vertical distribution of power in a tall building, follow a procedure similar to an indoor transformer siting. Where possible, run a vertical bus duct on a wall common to the elevator shaft, janitor closet, or corridor. In a factory, a bus duct run should be located away from operator positions.

Underfloor ducts. Individual conductors are usually installed in an underfloor duct system, and it is possible for the phase and

EC&M February 1995

FIGURE 8-1 (2 OF 3)

neutral conductors of a 2-wire branch circuit to be from 6 to 23 in. apart (depending on the cross section of the cell). This configuration would create significant magnetic fields. Recommended practice would be to twist the individual conductors of a branch circuit together in pairs. For a large new construction project, twisted cable assemblies can be purchased from specialty cable companies with only a slight increase in cost. At an existing installation, all the wires in the duct could be tie-wrapped at each outlet in the duct system.

What to watch out for

Wiring errors. When conductors are installed in such a way that circuit conductors are not in the same cable or raceway, substantial magnetic fields are created by the separated supply and return currents. The most common error is violating Sec. 250-23(a) by making a connection between a neutral and an equipment grounding conductor on the load side of the service disconnect; this usually happens at sub-panels. In this instance, neutral currents will flow on *both* the neutral and the equipment grounding conductor.

Other errors include incorrect wiring of 3-way switching circuits and the connection of neutrals from two different branch circuits at some point other than panel neutral busses, such as at junction boxes, switches, receptacles, etc.

Water pipe problems. Three specific areas can be addressed here.

• Neutral grounds to a water pipe on the load side of the service can cause problems similar to the case mentioned above, where Sec. 250-23(a) is violated by making a connection between a neutral and an equipment grounding conductor, on the load side of the service disconnect. If any electrical equipment, such as a hot water heater, is also connected to a metal water pipe, the water pipe will probably become a parallel path for current that should be flowing over the neutral.

• Physical damage or corrosion can cause the neutral conductor (often uninsulated) on an overhead service drop to open up, or sever. With this condition and with water supply laterals connected to conductive water mains, the water system can function as a parallel neutral. When this happens, unbalanced neutral currents seeking to return to the utility source will pass out of the building over the water lateral. They will return to the source after passing through the water main, a neigh-

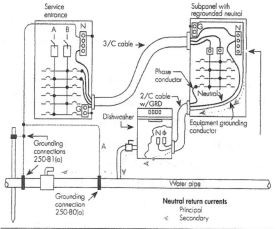

An example of a connection that allows a water pipe to function as a parallel neutral. The equipment grounding conductor run to the neutral bus of the subpanel is a violation of the NEC. This type of wiring error is widespread.

boring water lateral, and then through the neighboring service disconnect and out over the neighboring neutral.

• Currents can originate outside a building from the power company distribution system (typically, a looped primary circuit) or from neighboring buildings via the water service. An insulating coupling, or fitting, can be installed in the water service. However, it must be located *outside* of the premises, at least 10 ft from the building wall, per NEC Sec. 250-81(a).

Note that installing an insulating fitting in a water line to prevent the entry of currents has the disadvantage of decreasing ground conductivity, which under certain fault conditions may cause excess voltage to appear on plumbing fixtures and appliance enclosures. Thus, an insulating fitting can cause both a shock hazard and damage to an appliance that would not have occurred if there had been a connection to the water system.

However, a device called an automatic ground connector, which reconnects the ground in the event of a severe fault, is available. This device is similar in principle to a conventional surge arrester, but operates on a different voltage range. Because this is a new device that has not yet been tested by a recognized testing authority, approval from the local au-

thority having jurisdiction should be obtained.

When an insulating fitting is installed, a ground wire should be clamped beyond the fitting and extended back into the building. This allows the option of installing an automatic ground connector or reestablishing the ground in the future.

The importance of testing

Conducting a magnetic field survey upon completion of an installation in new construction is recommended. Such a survey can be done also at an existing location to detect long standing wiring errors or other abnormal conditions.

Two different types of meters are used. A single coil, or single axis, meter (about $235) determines the direction of the field and is useful for finding the field source. This type of meter can provide an approximate rms reading, but a calculation is required.

A 3-coil or 3-axis meter (about $1400) gives a true rms reading of fields from all directions and is not dependent on the orientation of the meter. Capable of making readings every 4 sec over a 24-hr period, this type of meter can be left at a site, or a person can carry it along a predetermined path. Accumulated data can be downloaded into a computer. •

FIGURE 8-1 (3 OF 3)

Public Speaking Opportunities

Almost any kind of speaking engagement enhances your image and credibility.

Teaching

Most professional organizations offer continuing education courses. It will enhance your reputation to arrange to be a guest lecturer.

The RI chapter of the Illuminating Engineering Society every couple of years offered either a basic lighting course or an advanced lighting course. Instruction was for three-hour sessions on eight nights. Not surprisingly (since I was the RI chapter's founding president), I was asked to be the instructor. I agreed to teach the first night and help select instructors for each of the other sessions. Eight lectures would have required a great deal of time and preparation. Also, in addition to giving me some publicity, it allowed me to help some of my contacts to get some notoriety. My lecture also gave me an opportunity to scope out some future employees.

Don't let yourself get roped into a multi-night teaching engagement at a local college. It's very time consuming with little benefit, poor pay, and (in most cases) no student appreciation.

New Service Lectures

Every time that you start a new service, try to be a guest speaker at any professional organization whose members might use your service or recommend you. We had a local mayor who had the reputation of being available to speak at the opening of an envelope; my criteria were not much higher. Prepare a PowerPoint presentation and hand out your announcement. If the organization does an actual mailing, try to get the program chairmen to enclose your announcement so those who don't come to the meeting will receive your information. At the meeting, don't pass out the announcement until after your lecture, because attendees may read it instead of listening to you. Take the opportunity to make new contacts.

Major Seminar

When something *dramatic* happens, seize the opportunity.

In 2003, we had a tragedy in Rhode Island. One hundred people perished in a fire at the Station nightclub. This catastrophic event was the impetus for a dramatic overhaul of our state fire code. The most revolutionary thing about this new code was that it was retroactive; the "grandfather clause" did not apply.

All existing buildings were required to meet the new code in accordance to a graduated implementation schedule.

I had recently been appointed to the RI Building Code Standards Committee and was too busy to take part in the overhaul of the fire code. But once it became law, I decided to put on a free seminar to educate fire officials and building owners of the new impact.

All my project managers were expert fire-alarm-system designers, and we had kept up with the proposed changes daily. But we spent a lot of time making sure that we understood which building types required which upgrade and the required timetable. I decided that my staff would be the panel of presenters and field the questions. I personally introduced our services with a PowerPoint presentation, describing the advantages of hiring a consulting engineering firm to design fire-alarm-system upgrades.

I rented the largest banquet hall at the fanciest, centrally located hotel in the state for a grand buffet breakfast meeting. We did a mailing to our mailing list and to the mailing lists of all the chambers of commerce throughout the state. We did radio advertisements (one-minute spots liberally mentioning our company name) starting ten days before the seminar. Note: Ethically, advertising by engineers is severely frowned upon, but these were public service announcements sponsored by an engineering firm, so not a problem. I had many sleepless nights wondering if we would make incompetent fools out of ourselves and provide breakfast to only a handful of fire officials.

We had over five hundred guests, and our seminar was an enormous success. It generated well over $1–2 million in fire-alarm-system design fees over the next five years and promoted other types of engineering work for us throughout New England.

I'm certainly not saying to take advantage of the misfortunes of others. But I am saying to look for opportunities, have the courage to proceed, and do it *first class*.

After the seminar, I mailed a new service announcement to all attendees and made a personal phone call to all who were potential clients. I thanked them for attending and inquiring about their needs. I also asked if they knew of anyone who might also need our services. If I got a referral, I always started the conversation by saying, "I'm calling at the request of _____." Always ask for the job.

OUTLINE GUIDE

- **Collect business cards:** Start a contact list, including both business and personal information.

- **Contact Form:** Create a form for each person on your list.

- **Note each contact:** Each time that you contact the person, list the date and details on this sheet.

- **Mailing List:** Expand your mailing list to include all the players in your industry.

- **Once you're in business:** I recommend a minimum of two mailings per year.

- **Newsletter:** One of your mailings each year should be a News Letter.

- **Articles:** Try to publish at least one article per year in the most prominent magazine in your industry.

- **Article topics:** Write about your projects or clients or timely issues in your industry.

- **Include:** A "headshot" photo of yourself and a brief biography.

- **Reprints:** Designing, printing and distributing reprints of your articles is one of the keys to being successful.

- **Distribution:** Send reprints to your entire mailing list regardless of their interest in the topic and include a copy with all future proposals irrespective of the type.

- **Public speaking:** Almost any kind of speaking engagement enhances your image and credibility.

What people are saying:

Included are more than 100 marketing methods. + I can't believe what great marketing ideas are included. + This book focuses on the top marketing ideas ever used. + These are the best small business tools for any profession. + I ordered two more as gift marketing ideas for my children. + This is one of the best sales and marketing books ever written. + This is a list of sales tools that I can choose from in the future.

CHAPTER 9

YOUR DISASTER RECOVERY PLAN

INTRODUCTION

Not many of us could have predicted the recent pandemic, and fewer of us have prepared a plan for our business to recover from it. We also need a business plan to recover from other kinds of business disasters, like fires or floods of our places of business. Some of us need to plan for natural disasters like hurricanes, blizzards, tornados, wildfires, avalanches, droughts, volcanos, or even tsunamis.

I suggest that you use this chapter as a guide in preparing "Your Disaster Recovery Plan" for your specific business. It will be a lot easier to leisurely develop it now rather than when your pants are on fire or you are learning the back stroke.

The document that you create is "*Your* Disaster Recovery Plan," so you need to decide what's best for your company. Just highlight the items that you like in this chapter and then create a separate list of your ideas. (Please don't share this document with your friends. Instead, advise them to buy my book from my website or on Amazon.)

To make creating a plan easier for others, I will provide a PDF of this chapter, available for download at a nominal price from my website: https://www.TheEngineersResource.com/shop.

The PDF can't be changed, but it can be highlighted, and then a separate list of ideas that apply to the specific business can be created.

The following is a summary of advice:
- Budget and prepare for adequate emergency funding
- Prepare "Your Emergency Contact Lists" *now*
- Pre-recovery "thanks and reassurance" to staff
- Keep staff informed and updated
- Protect property from further damage (if appropriate)
- Protect property from looting (if needed)
- Investigate your insurance coverage
- Repair property (if needed)
- Safeguard business records
- Notify, reassure, and continually update clients/customers
- Temporarily expand business online
- Search for and move to temporary space (if needed)
- Promote temporary reopening
- Promote permanent reopening
- Thank staff, workers, and customers for their efforts/understanding.

Preamble Regarding the Recent Pandemic

Before elaborating on each of the above, I propose we reflect on the impact of the recent past.

The coronavirus pandemic that hopefully is in the distant past by the time that you're reading this was a worldwide disaster and probably (hopefully) the most dramatic event any of us will experience in our lifetimes.

This incident will impact all of us permanently, each of us in different ways.
- The loss of someone we know and in some cases the loss of a friend or loved one
- The fear of closeness to others
  - When greeting a stranger, you may be reluctant to shake hands. Perhaps bowing or waving will become the norm.
  - When greeting family, "hugs" may no longer be common, or they'll be done with turned-away faces.
  - Kissing will become rare and reserved for the closest of relationships. Perhaps cheek touching or double cheek touching, like the French, may become common.

- Other effects of social isolation
  - Many of us have been alone throughout this ordeal. Will extroverts emerge as introverts? Will some never emerge?
  - Families who have been isolated together will be less affected and hopefully form closer bonds.
  - Many who have been on the front lines, like health-care workers, who have been exposed to great risks and possibly unspeakable horrors and may have had to isolate from their loved ones, may be the most affected, if they are fortunate enough to survive.
  - Those near the front lines may be affected, but perhaps to a lesser degree: store clerks, pharmacists, delivery people—just to name a few.

These are only a few of the concerns. But if you heed my advice and prepare "Your Disaster Recovery Plan" now, you will be better prepared for what the future may bring your way.

Now, let me elaborate on the checklist.

Implement Your "Emergency Funding" Plan

Instead of *frantically* calling "daddy" for emergency funds when your disaster occurs, plan ahead (or call him now).

First, budget your needs. This task is made more difficult because you don't know what kind of disaster that you will be experiencing, the duration of your business disruption, or if you'll be able to remain partially in operation. Make assumptions. Budget for your business to be totally closed for one month.

- Overhead—Include rent, utilities, insurance, loan payments, mortgage, and a multitude of other expenses.
- Materials and inventory—Cancel new shipments of materials to you, if possible.
- Payroll—If you can, plan to keep your entire staff employed for at least the first month.
- Taxes—You may be able to delay these. But with the red tape and possible late fees and penalties, avoid this, if possible.
- Your personal needs

Sources of revenue:
- Savings—Most owners of small businesses have enough personal savings to keep their businesses afloat for at least a month. But during

business downturns, your credit cards may be maxed out. A savvy business person would budget their business and personal expenses to have a minimum of three months operating capital readily available.

- Loans—Assume that you might need as much as three months operating capital during a personal or more widespread emergency and inquire about the likelihood of available funds for you, based on your banking relationship and credit worthiness. It might be prudent to arrange for a line of credit. But these are easily canceled by the lender on the spur of the moment, based on current circumstances or changes in their policies.
- Consider special opportunities—Government grants or low- or no-interest loans that might become excusable.
- Daddy—I smiled as I listed this item, and I certainly recommend that you make every effort to be self-sufficient. But if you failed to adequately save and you're not creditworthy, he may see loaning you money as a better alternative than having you and your spouse and kids move in with him.

The point is, in order to be financially prepared, you need to budget your expenses and potential sources of revenue and plan as best as you can. When a disaster happens, most people's first thought is, *How am I going to pay for this?* But if you plan ahead, you'll at least have your guesstimate.

Implement "Your Emergency Contact Lists"

Don't search for the right phone number or e-mail address while you're standing ankle deep in water or choking on smoke. Have "Your Emergency Contact List" ready and up-to-date to serve your immediate needs.

Print your list including business and (where possible) home numbers of the person assigned to your account. Give copies to your senior staff. Store numbers in your cell phone and direct your senior staff to do likewise.

Who should be included?
- Disaster-recovery specialist (primary and secondary alternates)
- Vendors (to cancel or modify deliveries)
- Security-alarm company
- Security-personnel company
- Sprinkler-repair company

- Plumber
- Electrician
- Fire-alarm service company
- Insurance agent
- For each policy, emergency contact numbers
- Window repair/replacement company
- General contractor
- Realtor
- Movers
- Sign-rental company
- Sign-repair company
- Website guy
- Media people
- Professional service companies (accountant, attorney, payroll, etc.)

Add other contacts that are necessary for the needs of your particular company, and be prepared to update and distribute as new sources develop. And include services that may help your employees meet their personal and family obligations.

Pre-recovery Thanks and Reassurance to Staff

Regardless of the particular type of tragedy that your business is experiencing, your staff, no doubt, will have immediately taken steps to protect your business. It is important to show them how much you appreciate their efforts on your behalf.

Staff also need reassurance regarding their future. Unfortunately, many among us are living from paycheck to paycheck. However, false assurance is never helpful. But without a plan, you would likely be at a loss for words.

Also, with a unique, new threat (like a pandemic), there are many unknowns. What is the extent of the problem? How long will it last? What government help will be available? What government restrictions will be imposed? What are your options?

But now you will have a *new tool*: "Your Disaster Recovery Plan." Keep copies of your plan readily available. (Not just in a file in your place of business that is burned out, flooded, or threatened by natural disasters.) And it's something that you should reread and update periodically (at least once a year).

I suggest initially telling your staff something like the following:

Thank you so much for your concern and help. For now, **everyone** is still on the payroll with their usual benefits. Working together, we'll figure this out.

Notice the elements to include in your statement:

- The first words are "Thank you."
- It includes a temporary assurance without making a "time" commitment.
- It emphasizes the word "everyone" instead of the words "For now."
- It implies that you don't yet have all of the answers.
- It states confidence in finding a solution.
- It is brief and concise.

Now compose your statement, write it down, and memorize it. You won't instill much confidence if you have to read it to your staff.

Keep Staff Informed and Updated

Depending upon what your business does, your staff may already be aware of the problem, but you need to make sure that they appreciate the full effect of the disaster.

- What actually happened
- Why it happened
- Steps that you are taking to mitigate negative effects
- How this disaster affects them personally

It's also important to give updates as the situation changes (which, during the pandemic, was almost daily).

Protect Property from Further Damage (if Appropriate)

If the problem is a pandemic, there's no damage, unless it is done later by protesters or looters.

If the problem is fire or water, call in the disaster-recovery specialists.

Years ago, I didn't even know that there were disaster-recovery companies. Two months after I bought a large apartment complex, I got a call late one afternoon from a tenant who complained of six inches of water in their apartment. My new on-site apartment manager had quit the week before, so I didn't have someone else to handle the problem, and I didn't know what to do. My engineering company's senior associate said, "Maybe this investment was a big mistake."

My office manager and our secretary agreed to help, and after gathering three wet-vacs, we traveled to the site. There, we discovered that there were six apartments that had flooded during a torrential downpour. I called my insurance agent, who provided the name of a local disaster-recovery company. They arrived within the hour and pumped out and cleaned the mess and shampooed the rugs. These companies only work on an hourly basis, but you should request an estimate as soon as feasible. I compensated each of the tenants for three days in a hotel (although some stayed in their damp apartment or with relatives), and I eventually had to install all new carpeting.

As it turned out, my problem was a blocked drain in the parking lot. My complex was built on a hill and water flowed down to the lower building, flooding the hall and seeping into the apartments. The permanent solution was to check the drains each fall and clean them out if necessary. Just to be sure, I added eight inches of concrete to each of the stair landings to make them a step height above the walks and force any floodwater to go around my building. I neglected to tell my downhill neighbors about my new stair landings. The lesson here is to call the professionals.

Protect Property from Damage by Persons (like Looters) (if Needed)

During the present pandemic, most rural areas have had few security issues. But some major cities have had significant problems.

Security is an issue that should be addressed for everyday business concerns, with further measures planned for in the event of a disaster.

It is up to each facility to balance security controls against risks, taking into account the costs along with broader issues such as aesthetics. Physical-access security measures that are appropriate for a prison are inappropriate in an office or most business facilities, although the principles are similar.

- Perimeter security
  - If you own the building housing your business, barriers such as fences, walls, and vehicle barriers act as the outermost layer of security. But most businesses don't need any of these.
- Physical-entry security to consider
  - Security shutter
  - Entry doors and window upgrades
  - Security hardware (locks, bolts, etc.)
- Security lighting
- Intrusion detection and electronic surveillance

- Video surveillance
- Access control
- Security personnel
  - Most businesses don't need on-site security personnel. But during the threat of looting, this could be a consideration. It might be a good idea to find a trustworthy company that provides security personnel, and discuss possible needs and associated costs on a temporary basis. What are the options/recommendations? An armed guard at the front door, and at the rear door, and another patrolling around the building, and/or inside? Can they add you to their priority customer list? There may be concerns, both pro and con, regarding your liability for using or not using security personnel.
- Fire protection
  - If you are building a new building, sprinklers may be required by code. If you are buying or leasing an existing building, they're an asset. Consider not only the value of your building, furnishings, and merchandise but also the value of preserving records.
- Fire alarms
  - Fire-alarm systems are primarily people protection and not property protection. The local fire/building codes dictate the minimum requirements. But fire-alarm systems can provide early notification to the fire department and possibly greatly reduce property damage. (See chapter 8 for an example concerning the "Station Nightclub" fire in RI in 2003.)

My recommendations:

First consider your needs on an everyday basis. Then separately evaluate upgrades that may be needed during a disaster. Look at the previous list and take into consideration things like your location and its history of crime, your budget, and common sense. Call your insurance company and discuss your liability. Perhaps call a security-alarm company and arrange for them to visit your facility to make recommendations. Sometimes options are more economical than you may first think, and security advisors may have recommendations concerning other security improvements that you hadn't considered, even things beyond their usual area of expertise.

Investigate Your Insurance Coverage

Riot damage is generally covered by business insurance policies under theft and fire. Moreover, certain policies may also offer provision for businesses whose trade is adversely affected by riots, even if this is not as a direct result of damage or looting. Ask your insurance agent about this now. Perhaps extra coverage can be added at little cost.

Also, take this opportunity to discuss other disasters (fire and flood, for example).

My friend Mark from the Pelican Café was kind enough to review a draft of this new chapter for me. He had the following advice to offer:

> The first person I called was our insurance agent. We have business-disruption insurance like a lot of other companies. What everyone found out, and the president mentioned on TV early on, was that they excluded viruses from these policies. So we weren't eligible, along with the many consumers who had booked cruises. The president called out the insurance companies on this topic, and hopefully, the language will be revised in policies moving forward.

Repair Property (if Needed)

When there's no longer an emergency, repair the damage.

Of course, the extent of the damage will dictate the means needed for repairs. If you have broken windows, call a window guy—not a general contractor.

If you are part of a hurricane, riot, or pandemic, your options for repairs may be limited. If the disaster you are experiencing is a "personal" problem (i.e., a pipe broke and flooded your office space), you will have more choices available.

But if you need a contractor, hire a licensed and insured contractor. Seek a recommendation from someone that you trust before interviewing contractors. Meet separately with at least two to view the damage together and discuss options, schedule, guarantees, and their insurance coverage.

Safeguard Business Records

In today's age of computers and automatic saving to the cloud, preserving records is less of an issue than it once was. I download all of my documents to a portable hard drive every evening before going to bed. It takes less than five minutes, and I don't have to sit and watch its progress. I also have a second portable hard drive that I keep at a separate location. I download all files to this on the first of each month. (You didn't know that Jack was paranoid, did you?) Recently, my computer got hacked. Since then, I've created a separate file on my portable hard drive that I named *Private Documents*. I downloaded my password list, net-worth statement, and other personal documents to this file. Then I deleted these documents (including superseded copies) from my computer.

The internet represents an insecure channel for exchanging information, which leads to a high risk of intrusion or fraud, such as phishing, online viruses, Trojans, worms, and more. Many methods can be used to protect the transfer of data, including encryption. However, most companies need only a good antivirus software program. Also available are what are referred to as *security suites* that include firewalls, antivirus, antispyware, and more. These threats may become more prevalent during disasters, but are also an everyday concern. Make sure that your computers and network systems are adequately protected.

Keeping your computers properly functioning during a disaster is critical to the continuity of the operation of your business. Make sure that you have a reliable and competent service that can remotely access your computer and correct issues, if needed.

An electrical contractor friend of mine had to completely rebuild after a devastating fire. At the time, because his was a small building, sprinklers were not required by code, but he installed them anyway when he rebuilt. (Lessons learned.) He also installed a large, walk-in, fireproof vault for records, and staff would roll their file cabinet into the vault upon leaving for the day.

Retrieve any handwritten and any other nonelectronically stored records as soon as feasible.

Notify, Reassure, and Continually Update Clients/Customers
Communication in any disaster is important to business continuation.

With central coordination, working remotely is possible for most businesses. As soon as possible, notify clients/customers that you are still ready and able to serve their needs and how to get directly in touch with the person/department in your company who's handling their account. Bear in mind, with a national emergency, the National Guard may be activated and some staff may not be available for the duration. If so, reassign their duties and have the new person contact the client/customer personally to inform of their availability.

As the situation improves continue to reassure clients/customers.

If the crisis extends, provide newsletters offering helpful advice for coping with the problem and for eventual recovery.

It might be appropriate for a restaurant to e-mail "daily specials" to all customers. Even "Early Bird" discounts might work.

The important thing is that customers don't forget you and start doing business with one of your competitors.

Temporarily Expand Business Online

Most businesses are already offering some of their services and products on the internet. During a disaster, it's time to step up your online marketing.

During the recent pandemic, Realtors and car dealerships are offering "virtual tours" of their inventories.

Realtors offer videos showing interior views like virtual room-by-room, walk-through tours of their properties, including the exteriors, creating an experience simulating what a prospect would encounter in person, including persuasive narration. And now, some are even showing drone flyovers of not only their property, but also the associated neighborhood, local parks, schools, and points of interest.

Car dealerships are doing more than just showing pictures of their vehicles alongside spec sheets. Some are showing videos of a virtual tour of their showrooms, including each individual vehicle with under-the-hood views and all with full-audio narration (as if you were in their showroom) alongside a slick salesman. (But a virtual salesman who can't slip your wallet out of your back pocket.) Now you can even buy online and accept home delivery of your fully sanitized vehicle without coming in contact with another person or visiting the dealership.

Most upscale, eat-in restaurants have been closed. I am usually making an effort to keep my weight down, but my one "splurge" for the week on Saturdays has been a short stack of the *absolute best* blueberry pancakes anywhere, at the Pelican Café in Lake Park, Florida. This is one of the things that I have missed most during this period of isolation. I also miss talking with the owners Mark & Karen, being greeted by the lovely hostesses Mary or Carol, and being cared for by my favorite waitress, Carolyn.

But while writing this article, I checked their website and found to my surprise:

> For the safety and convenience of our valued customers, the Pelican Café is now offering curbside pickup and home delivery within a ten-mile radius.

Jack is having pancakes this Saturday! Yum! (Actually, I'm not waiting. I'm calling right now.)

If they have an e-mail or a phone number list, now is the time to promote this new availability.

With a little ingenuity, most businesses can figure out a way to stay open during most disasters.

Search for and Move to Temporary Space (if Needed)

If your place of business is only partially damaged, perhaps you could move your operations to other rooms, even if your customers have to temporarily use a rear entrance. If some employees temporarily worked from home, the remaining space might be enough for your on-site needs.

If your workspace is completely unusable, you may have to move, at least temporarily. If you don't own the building, a permanent move may be appropriate. Even if you do own your building, it might be feasible to permanently move and later repair and sell or lease your present property.

The ease of relocation depends a lot on your type of business and availability of properties. If you need general office space, there's always a supply. Restaurant space is likely to be more difficult. However, there may be a local closed restaurant that suits your needs, including equipment and furnishings.

I recommend working with an established local Realtor (not just an agent or your cousin Vinnie from another city).

Most commercial properties are leased on a long-term basis, usually three years or more. However, some properties that are less in demand are quite flexible, if pressed. Take the time, investigate all possibilities, negotiate the best deal, and carefully read the lease, if one is to be signed. Also, remember that leases are double-edged swords. They lock you in for the term, but also lock down the lessor's responsibilities.

If customers/clients are not coming into your business, less space may be required.

Don't let your employees become your moving men; hire professional movers. You don't want to assume the liability for the possibility of injury to your staff or damage to your equipment.

Don't delay repairs to your permanent property while you are busy finding/occupying new temporary space. Also, don't assume that your landlord is making repairs that meet your standards and that the work is progressing as quickly as can be accomplished.

Promote Temporary Reopening

As soon as you are ready to temporarily reopen, obviously, it is time to inform potential customers of your availability.

- Modify signage
- Make changes to your website
- Consider radio/TV/newspaper ads
- Consider direct-mail marketing
- Start e-mail marketing (your list +/or a purchase list)

Modify Signage

Potential costumers driving/walking by your facility need some indication that you are open. Perhaps your usual sign can easily be modified. If not, rental companies often offer portable signs with clip-on letters allowing your personal, detailed message. On a temporary emergency basis, it may be acceptable to even place the sign on the sidewalk or in the parking lane in the street, as long as pedestrian traffic is not impeded. Tip – Check your temporary sign frequently. Pranksters sometimes make embarrassing modifications.

Make Changes to Your Website

Surprisingly, over a month into the pandemic many upscale local restaurants had not changed their websites, even though they were offering curbside and delivery.

I am reluctant to keep mentioning the Pelican Café, but they did a so-much-better job in modifying their website than any other that I could find. Here's what the top of their home page looked like a few weeks into the pandemic. (Black-and-white reproductions don't adequately depict the elegance and three dimensional feel displayed. Visit: https://www.thepelicancafe.com/ for a "live" view.)

For the safety and convenience of our valued customers, Pelican Cafe is now offering Curbside Pick-up and Home Delivery within a 10 mile radius.

BRUNCH: Tues. - Sat. 11am - 2pm
DINNER: Tues. - Sat.   4pm - 8pm
Please Call Ahead. Phone Orders Only.
561-842-7272

BRUNCH MENU
DINNER MENU

As always, we are adhering to the highest of safety standards and are adopting a responsible social distancing approach. (Although we really want to give you a hug!)

On Easter Saturday, April 11, 2020, the following appeared at the top of the main page:

Enjoy Pelican Café in the comfort of your home on Easter Sunday.

561-843-7272

Kindly call to place your order by Friday April 10 or Saturday April 11 to ensure proper Easter delivery or pickup time.

DINNER MENU

EASTER SPECIALS

We'll be open on Easter Sunday for Curbside Pickup & Free Home Delivery from 11am–4pm.

Mark, one of the owners, was a marketing professional in corporate for twenty-five years. So it's no wonder that he did a great job. But with some serious effort, you can produce decent results. However, turning to a marketing professional might be a good investment for your business.

Offer Curbside Delivery

This seems to me to be the easiest option. But, the problem is that people are lazy and reluctant to go out in the best of times. During a disaster, like a pandemic, people are frightened to leave home. But, make sure that your potential customers are aware of this option if available.

Offer Home Delivery

If you already offer home delivery, you already have this up and running. If not, there are three choices: hire delivery people, use your own staff, or use a delivery service.

If you hire delivery people, make sure that they have a valid driver's license, a good driving record, and can provide proof of insurance. Check with your insurance agent to be sure that you are insured in case your employee gets into a serious accident or commits a crime.

If your staff makes deliveries, you still have the previous concerns, but you avoid hiring someone new and this would be a good way to keep your wait/bus staff employed.

Hiring a delivery service avoids the above concerns but makes layoffs among your existing staff more likely.

Consider Radio/TV/Newspaper Ads

Perhaps you already have a media advertising campaign that you use on an ongoing basis, or seasonally or just on occasion. Possibly you can add an introduction to your present ads to highlight the circumstances of your current disaster. Also, if the disaster is shared by your customers, prominently including an advice article might help customers and generate good-will for you. A "Coronavirus Update," for example. But, rather than cluttering up your home page. I suggest something like this: For a Coronavirus Update [click here].

If media advertising is new to you, most media outlets will be happy to help you while generating income for their company. But don't let panic cause your spending to be too aggressive.

Consider Direct-Mail Marketing

Marketing mailing lists are available by zip codes. They usually can be sorted by biographics (20–30-year-olds, for example). But beware: some lists are out of date and/or unreliable. There are usually special postal rates for bulk mailing within a single zip code. Also, check on weight restrictions. You may be able to send out three pieces for the same postal rate (an explanation letter, a menu, and a coupon.) Remember: most mailing lists are rented on a one-use basis.

A call to a local advertising agency might provide other ideas and even garner a reference for a reliable list seller or you can usually rent through them at no additional cost because they buy at an agency discount.

Start E-mail Marketing (Your List +/or Purchase List)

Most savvy merchants have developed their own customer lists over time. Even your list of telephone numbers or mailing addresses can be converted to an e-mail list with a little ingenuity (a call or letter offering a discount coupon, if they e-mail a request, for example).

Again, in some cases e-mail lists are available with some of the same restrictions as for mailing lists. E-mail lists are usually much shorter than mailing lists, but still may be worth considering. Make it part of your "Disaster Recovery Plan" to start accumulating an e-mail list of your own now. With every receipt that you give a customer include a "Valuable Coupon" that says, "To activate this coupon, e-mail the word *activate* to YourCo.Name@YourEmailAddress.com."

My friend Mark from the Pelican Café was kind enough to provide the following advice:

> Social Media plays a vital role in communications during disasters. It is important to tap into media partners support (i.e., CBS has a *We're Open* link, the Women's Chamber of Commerce forwarded our e-mail to all members, *Florida Weekly* has a 90K subscriber list that we tapped into, Facebook has a new group named *The Socially Distanced Supper Club*, etc.). It is important to take the time to learn and stay current in our ever evolving digital age. Marketing will always be critically important to any brands sustainability.
>
> Also, give back, especially in times of disaster. You always stand taller with someone else on your shoulders.

Promote Permanent Reopening

Be prepared for the crush! At least, that's what we hope. But my mantra is "It doesn't just happen. You make it happen."

The following checklist should look familiar:

- Modify signage
- Make changes to your website
- Consider radio/TV/newspaper ads
- Consider direct-mail marketing
- Start e-mail marketing (your list +/or a purchase list)

The same principles apply to your grand reopening that applied to your temporary reopening.

Beginning a week to ten days before, modify your signage to announce your grand reopening on [day and date]. If convenient, pick the first of the month or a holiday to help people remember, and don't forget to include the name of the day of the week. Hang balloons from your sign for the first week. Rent a clown costume and hire someone to dance around out front, whatever it takes to attract customers.

Many years ago, I bought a block of defaulted condos from the FDIC, after the condo-conversion bubble burst. I hired a professional clown to be at the nearest main intersection every Sunday during open house. My condos were on the wrong side of the border between a desirable neighborhood and a less desirable one. At the intersection, there was a fifteen-foot-long sign proclaiming "Welcome to the Less Desirable City," with an arrow pointing toward my condos. From a sign company, I had two fifteen-foot-banner signs made proclaiming "Happy Holidays" and had them hung on both sides of the city sign, and it wasn't until March that someone removed them. It doesn't just happen. You make it happen.

While you are temporarily reopened, work with your website designer and your media advertising people so that you can seamlessly update everything on the day of the grand reopening.

Seven to ten days before the grand reopening, announce it on all of your media channels.

Most cities have business talk shows. These work well if you're prepared. The first thing you need to do is convince the station's news director that you're offering useful and entertaining information. Don't wing it; prepare. Prepare a letter addressed to the news director and make your best arguments about why *they* would like you to come on their show, not why *you* want to be interviewed. Prepare your arguments on your computer in letter form. It may be necessary to actually send a letter or e-mail if you aren't able to speak with the right person or if a letter is requested. This will also force you to research the correct person and know his or her title, mailing address, and perhaps that person's resume. Unlike a request to publish your article, this offer can be extended to several media outlets at once. Why not get two or three times the benefit out of this preparation?

Make a concise list of benefits that your interview will bring to the station and its listeners/viewers. And, for each, prepare some bullet points to support your assertions. It should be a single page (300–500 words). Practice delivering your message; if you don't practice, you'll sound like you're reading it.

Immediately upon being accepted for an interview, e-mail a suggested question list to the interviewer, as a guide. If they get your list before preparing theirs, he or she can go home early, and you're going to be asked the questions for which you're best prepared. Also, include an introduction: the exact words that you want the interviewer to use to introduce you. And include your detailed bio that will hopefully help to establish your credibility. Next, prepare your list of answers in a somewhat informal tone, commit them to memory, and practice. Try to think of questions that might be asked that weren't on the list that you provided. (How often do you beat your wife? If a question similar to this seems at all likely in your case, don't do interviews.)

If you have partners, choose the most outgoing and well-spoken to be the voice and face of your company. Alternatively, you and your significant other (if you're both involved in the business) might make an interesting combination. I advise against having a non-owner as the spokesperson for your company. I cringe every time that I see the ads for a national phone company being hyped by the previous spokesperson for a competitor.

Your e-mail blasts should hype reopening, and you should offer specials with coupons that expire two weeks after reopening so that they don't gather dust. And don't forget: if your advertising is general (not to a specific customer/client), be sure to include the requirement that they send an e-mail to you to activate any coupon. (And don't forget to add this new potential customer/client to your contact list.)

If you tried direct-mail marketing during your temporary reopening and it worked well for you, it may be worth considering again. However, the customers/clients that were attracted back then are already on board or off board. If you decide to try it again, you are expected to rent the list a second time and proper timing depends upon the reliability of the mail delivery.

Reaching your goal of restoring your business to full operation will be the net sum of successes and failures. Taking your best shot at *each* effort improves your chances of accomplish the desired result.

Thank Staff, Workers, and Customers for Their Efforts/Understanding

As soon as you catch your breath, there's one last step to complete.

Start by composing a personal letter to each category of person who has helped you and your business get through this ordeal. Try to avoid being too emotional/sappy.

Don't send the letter to your staff. Talk to them privately as a group. Avoid singling out individuals, except perhaps in a general way. Later, privately thank individuals for certain special efforts.

Thank the contracted workers in person and follow through by sending a personal letter to each of their companies. But choose your words carefully because your letter may be posted at the company office or used in their advertising.

Consider a party for staff and workmen. If funds are tight, soft drinks and munchies would still be appreciated.

Next, e-mail a thank-you note to your customers. Assuming that these messages are all part of the same e-mail blast, they should be somewhat general. Instead of saying, "Thank you so much for coming for curbside delivery or for ordering home deliver" substitute "We are thankful to all of our loyal customers, many of whom have ordered home delivery during this crisis and some who have even driven here for curbside pickup."

Jack's Final Advice
Before the recent past fades from your memory, take the time to update "Your Disaster Recovery Plan" to include "lessons learned."

"Genius GIFT Idea for you !"
Gift a copy of this book to business people who have
helped you through the recent crises.
Here are the benefits:
- ✓ The "Your Disaster Recovery Plan" chapter will help them develop a Business Plan for their particular business to recover from any future disaster including fires or floods of their places of business, or weather disasters.
- ✓ The "Marketing" advice will help their businesses thrive in both good and bad times.
- ✓ Your personal message on the inside cover will remind them of who was thoughtful enough to give them this timely and helpful present.

Go to my website to see "QUANTITY DISCOUNTS":
https://www.TheEngineersResource.com/shop

(SEE APPENDIX)
Fortunately, many businesses have "stepped-up" and quickly modified their websites and practices to cope with the new reality. In the APPENDIX I have included some of the best examples that I was able to find on company websites. Perhaps, these will spark some ideas regarding your promotional needs. [Note: None of the businesses sited in this book have endorsed me or my book in any way and are not receiving compensation for the use.]

OUTLINE GUIDE

- **Implement Your "Emergency Funding" Plan**
  Budget costs for your business to be totally closed for one month.
  - Overhead, materials, and inventory, payroll, taxes, and your personal needs

  Sources of revenue:
  - Savings, loans, special opportunities, daddy—?

- **Implement "Your Emergency Contact Lists"**
  Who should be included?
  - Disaster-recovery specialist (primary and secondary alternates), vendors, security-alarm company, security-personnel company, sprinkler-repair company, plumber, electrician, fire-alarm service company, insurance agent, and for each policy—emergency contact numbers, window repair/replacement company, general contractor, Realtor, movers, sign-rental company, sign-repair company, website guy, media people, professional service companies (accountant, attorney, payroll, etc.)

- **Pre-recovery Thanks and Reassurance to Staff**
  - Thank you so much for your concern and help. For now, **everyone** is still on the payroll with their usual benefits. Working together, we'll figure this out.

- **Keep Staff Informed and Updated**
  - What actually happened
  - Why it happened
  - Steps that you are taking to mitigate negative effects
  - How this disaster affects them personally

- **Protect Property from Further Damage** (if Appropriate)
  - If the problem is a pandemic, there's no damage, unless it is done later by looters.
  - If the problem is fire or water, call in the "disaster-recovery specialists."

- **Protect Property from Damage by Persons** (like Looters) (if Needed)
  Consider each of the following:

- Perimeter security, physical-entry security, security lighting, intrusion detection, and electronic surveillance, video surveillance, access control, security personnel, fire protection (sprinklers), fire alarms.

- **Investigate Your Insurance Coverage**
  - Riot damage is generally covered by business insurance policies under theft and fire.
  - Business-disruption insurance has always excluded viruses. This may change by the time that this book is published.

- **Repair Property** (if Needed)
  - When there is no longer an emergency, repair the damage.
  - Use the right licensed and insured contractor.

- **Safeguard Business Records**
  - Back up to the cloud and/or a portable hard drive.
  - Get a good antivirus software program or a suite including firewalls, antivirus, antispyware, and more.
  - Use a reliable and competent service that can remotely access your compute for repairs, if needed.
  - Retrieve any handwritten or nonelectronically stored records as soon as feasible.

- **Notify, Reassure, and Continually Update Clients/Customers**
  - Communication in any disaster is important to business continuation.
  - Make reassignments to cover for possibly missing staff.
  - As the situation improves, continue to reassure clients/customers.
  - If the crisis extends, provide newsletters offering helpful advice.
  - Don't let customers/clients forget you.

- **Temporarily Expand Business Online**
  - Step up your online marketing.
  - Car dealerships and Realtors should consider virtual tours of their inventory with full-audio narration.
  - Upscale restaurants should consider curbside pickup and home delivery within a ten-mile radius.

- **Search for and Move to Temporary Space** (if Needed)
  - Work with an established local Realtor.
  - Carefully read the lease.
  - Don't let your employees become your movers.
  - Don't assume that your landlord is making needed repairs.

- **Promote temporary reopening**
  - Modify signage
  - Make changes to your website
  - Consider radio/TV/newspaper ads
  - Consider direct-mail marketing
  - Start e-mail marketing (your list +/or a purchase list)

Consider radio/TV/newspaper ads

- Possibly, you can add an introduction to your present ads.
- Prominently including an advice article.

Consider direct-mail marketing

- Marketing "mailing lists" are available by zip codes.
- A call to a local advertising agency might provide other ideas.

Start e-mail marketing (your list +/or purchase list)

- Your list of telephone numbers or mailing addresses can be easily converted to an e-mail list. A call or letter offering a discount coupon, if they e-mail a request.
- With every receipt that you give a customer include a "Valuable Coupon" that says, "To activate this coupon, e-mail the word *activate* to...."
- Social media plays a vital role in communications during disasters.

Give back, especially in times of disaster.

- **Promote Permanent Reopening**
  - Modify signage
  - Make changes to your website
  - Consider radio/TV/Newspaper ads
  - Consider direct-mail marketing
  - Start E-mail marketing (your list +/or a purchase list)

The same principles apply as did to your temporary reopening.

- Hang balloons from your sign for the first week.
- Hire someone to dance around out front, whatever it takes to attract customers.
- Announce grand reopening on all of your media channels.
- Appear on business talk shows.
- Your e-mail blasts should hype reopening include the requirement for them to send an e-mail to you to activate any coupon (to expand your e-mail list).
- Taking your best shot at *each* effort, improves your chances of accomplish your desired result.

- **Thank Staff, Workers, and Customers for Their Efforts/Understanding**
  - As soon as you catch your breath, there is one more last step to complete.
  - Start by composing a personal letter to each category of person who helped.
  - Talk to your staff privately as a group.
  - Thank the workers in person.
  - Follow through by sending a personal letter to each of their companies.
  - Consider a party for staff and workers.
  - Next, e-mail a thank-you note to your customers.
  - Update "Your Disaster Recovery Plan" to include "lessons learned."

What people are saying:

Included are more than 100 marketing methods. + I can't believe what great marketing ideas are included. + This book focuses on the top marketing ideas ever used. + These are the best small business tools for any profession. + I ordered two more as gift marketing ideas for my children. + This is one of the best sales and marketing books ever written. + This is a list of sales tools that I can choose from in the future.

C H A P T E R   1 0

CONCLUSIONS

INTRODUCTION

We all want to be admired and looked up to by others. I always wanted to be more good looking and taller. But some things can't be changed. However, while traveling by plane recently, I stood to allow a couple to take the two seats next to me, and when I did, I noticed how short they both were. At the end of the flight, I said: "I want to thank you. I have always wished I was taller and, thanks to you both, during this flight it felt like I accomplished that goal." My point is that I didn't actually need to be taller to perceive that I was taller. You are what you're perceived to be.

Most of us would like to be perceived as the smartest person in the room. If you really are, God bless you. If not, follow my advice, and you'll be perceived to be the smartest person in the room.

Creating this perception requires considerable effort and can be done in many ways. Your chances for success will be increased by employing several of the methods described herein.

OUTLINE GUIDE

- **Plan ahead:** Don't stumble into your career. Plan for it.

- **Your career choice:** Should be lucrative enough to support you and a family, not restrict where you can live, and not require odd hours or excessive travel.

- **Shadow**: Spend a day with someone in the field that interests you.

- **Owning a business:** Make a list of advantages and disadvantages.
  - Advantages: Making all the final decisions; never being laid-off; keeping all the profits; and being able to sell an asset upon retirement.
  - Disadvantages: Personal and family sacrifices; difficulty of dealing with employees and acceptance of any losses.

- **Visit the website** https://www.bls.gov/ooh:. The *Occupational Outlook Handbook* by the US Bureau of Labor Statistics for more career guidance.

- **My recommendation:** Choose to be a professional and own your own business.

- **Your job search:** Prepare a resume; check websites of potential employers; dress for success; and make follow-up calls.

- **Prepare for your interview:** Make a list of your skills, a list of anticipated questions with answers; and a list of your questions. Also, send a thank-you email.

- **Start the job right:** Be exceptional; start a notebook; and start writing white papers.

- **Get known:** Attend meetings of local industry organizations. Here you'll meet the players in your profession/industry, people who will be your colleagues, future competitors, or future employees.

- **Start a contact list:** including both business and personal information.

- **Become an officer:** Volunteer for committees and after you become accepted, let it be known that you want to be an officer.

- **Win awards:** After you have been active in an organization, nominate another involved member for an award and they will later return the favor. Or have a mutual friend suggest it.

- **Start saving:** You'll need equity, good credit, and banking relations to start a business.

- **It doesn't just happen.** You make it happen.

- **Business announcement.** Make your business announcement outstanding. It should look like a wedding invitation on fine thick paper with raised letters.

- **Letterhead and business cards.** Create elegant letterhead and business cards. Parchment with raised letters and no logo would be a good choice.

- **Brochure.** Your brochure is the face of the company. It will evolve as your firm grows. Try to make it versatile and something that will make you proud and distinguish you from your competitors.

- **Announcements.** Don't forget to send out announcements of awards, new services/specialties, and anniversaries.

- **Always consider public speaking opportunities**. This is especially important when you're trying to promote a new service or new specialty.

- **Seize an opportunity.** When something dramatic happens, be ready to act. I am certainly not saying to take advantage of the misfortunes of others. But I am saying to look for opportunities, have the courage to proceed, and do it *first class*.

- **Send notes.** Never forget to send thank you notes, and look for opportunities to send notes of congratulations. You don't even need to know someone to recognize their achievements.

- **Open houses and parties.** These are great ways to thank your clients, show off your celebrity clients, and tell all about new specialties and exciting projects.

- **Your notebook:** to record information, such as office procedures, your contact list, formulas, calculations, definitions, and anything that you might need again. Your lap-top will be your notebook.

- **Spend time:** Reading magazines in your industry, plus articles regarding business trends, and current affairs.

- **Success:** Includes: happiness, wealth, respect, good health, family and friends, interests, and charity.

- **Starting point of success:** Is happiness and not wealth. But wealth should not be overlooked.

- **Make a prioritized list:** Of your own ideas of the components of success.

- **White paper:** A white paper is a report or guide to help readers to understand an issue.

- **Memorize:** After you have prepared a white paper, reread it several times, and commit much of the information to memory.

- **Other uses:** White papers will serve as a useful future reference and possibly the basis of a magazine article authored by you.

- **New topics:** Investigate new topics of the day in your industry, write a white paper and offer new services regarding the subject matter.

- **How to write a white paper:**
  - Search for information
  - Highlight relevant data
  - Introduction/summary (conversationally)
  - Why the topic is important
  - Details
  - Close

- **Expert witness:** If you serve as an expert witness, white papers will help you to prepare for your report, deposition, testimony and cross-examination.

- **Starting a conversation:** Let the circumstances of the meeting determine the start of the conversation.

- **Encourage the other person to speak:** If the other person speaks two-thirds of the time, they will rate *you* as a great conversationalist.

- **Prepare a conversation statement:** Make a list of things about you and questions that you should ask.

- **Topics that you might include:** About me, books, movies, concerts, travel, and hobbies.

- **Memorize:** Try to commit most of your conversation statement to memory. If you keep referring to your notes, you won't look smart.

- **Priority:** Asking about the person that you're meeting is paramount.

- **Memory lists:** Will simplify your life and make others think that you're smart.

- **Don't reinvent the wheel:** Each time that you do a task that you know you'll repeat, make a list to make the task easier, next time.

- **Collect business cards:** Start a contact list, including both business and personal information.

- **Contact form:** Create a form for each person on your contact list.

- **Note each contact:** Each time that you contact the person, list the date and details on this sheet.

- **Mailing list:** Expand your mailing list to include all the players in your industry.

- **Once you're in business:** I recommend a minimum of two mailings per year.

- **Newsletter:** One of your mailings each year should be a newsletter.

- **Articles:** Try to publish at least one article per year in the most prominent magazine in your industry.

- **Article topics:** Write about your projects or clients or timely issues in your industry.

- **Include:** A headshot photo of yourself and a brief biography.

- **Reprints:** Designing, printing, and distributing reprints of your articles is one of the keys to being successful.

- **Distribution:** Send reprints of your articles to your entire mailing list regardless of their interest in the topic and include a copy with all future proposals irrespective of the type.

- **Public speaking:** Almost any kind of speaking engagement enhances your image and credibility.

Every business needs a "Disaster Recovery Plan". Not only for an unexpected event like a pandemic, but also for a plan to recover from other kinds of business disasters, like fires or floods of our places of business. Some of us need to plan for natural disasters like hurricanes, blizzards, tornados, wildfires, avalanches, droughts, volcanos, or even tsunamis.

Prepare "Your Disaster Recovery Plan" for your specific business today. It will be a lot easier to leisurely develop it, rather than when your pants are on fire or you are standing in 6" of water.

- **Implement Your "Emergency Funding" Plan**
  Budget costs for your business to be totally closed for one month. Try to allow for three months.
  - Overhead, materials, and inventory, payroll, taxes, and your personal needs
  Sources of revenue:
  - Savings, loans, special opportunities, daddy—?

- **Implement "Your Emergency Contact Lists"**
  Who should be included?
  - Disaster-recovery specialist (primary and secondary alternates), vendors, security-alarm company, security-personnel company,

sprinkler-repair company, plumber, electrician, fire-alarm service company, insurance agent, and for each policy—emergency contact numbers, window repair/replacement company, general contractor, Realtor, movers, sign-rental company, sign-repair company, website guy, media people, professional service companies (accountant, attorney, payroll, etc.)

- **Pre-recovery Thanks and Reassurance to Staff**

  Thank you so much for your concern and help.

  For now, **everyone** is still on the payroll with their usual benefits. Working together, we'll figure this out.

- **Keep Staff Informed and Updated**

- **Protect Property from Further Damage (if Appropriate)**

- **Protect Property from Damage by Persons (like Looters) (if Needed)**

- **Investigate Your Insurance Coverage**

- **Repair Property (if Needed)**

- **Safeguard Business Records**

- **Notify, Reassure, and Continually Update Clients/Customers**

- **Temporarily Expand Business Online**

- **Search for and Move to Temporary Space (if Needed)**

- **Promote temporary reopening**
  - Modify signage
  - Make changes to your website
  - Consider radio/TV/newspaper ads
  - Consider direct-mail marketing
  - Start e-mail marketing (your list +/or a purchase list)
  - Consider radio/TV/newspaper ads
  - Consider direct-mail marketing
  - Start e-mail marketing (your list +/or purchase list)
  - Your list of telephone numbers or mailing addresses can be easily converted to an e-mail list. A call or letter offering a discount coupon, if they e-mail a request.

- With every receipt that you give a customer include a "Valuable Coupon" that says, "To activate this coupon, e-mail the word *activate* to...."

- **Promote Permanent Reopening**

  The same principles apply as did to your temporary reopening.
  - Hang balloons from your sign for the first week.
  - Hire someone to dance around out front, whatever it takes to attract customers.
  - Announce grand reopening on all of your media channels.
  - Appear on business talk shows.
  - Your e-mail blasts should hype reopening include the requirement for them to send an e-mail to you to activate any coupon (to expand your e-mail list).
  - Taking your best shot at *each* effort, improves your chances of accomplish your desired result.

- **Thank Staff, Workers, and Customers for Their Efforts/ Understanding**
  - As soon as you catch your breath, this is the one more step to complete.
  - Update "Your Disaster Recovery Plan" to include "lessons learned."

What people are saying:

Included are more than 100 marketing methods. + I can't believe what great marketing ideas are included. + This book focuses on the top marketing ideas ever used. + These are the best small business tools for any profession. + I ordered two more as gift marketing ideas for my children. + This is one of the best sales and marketing books ever written. + This is a list of sales tools that I can choose from in the future.

WHY IS THIS IMPORTANT?

The more Amazon reviews I can get posted, my book moves up the rankings faster and gets promoted by Amazon under the "books you also might like" section.

Reviews also increase book sales. Many reviews would create serious momentum for my book rankings.

The bottom line: Reviews convince browsers to buy. Amazon will rank my book higher as well if there is activity taking place.

HOW TO POST A BOOK REVIEW ON AMAZON

- Go to Amazon.com.
- At the top of the screen, to the left of the search bar, the word *all* appears. Click on it and select *book* from the drop-down menu.
- Then type into the search bar the title of this book: *The Complete Guide to Marketing*. If the title pops up, click on it. Otherwise, click on the little magnifying glass on the right of the search bar.
- Several books will appear. Scroll down until you see my book, and click on the cover.

- Scroll (way down past other books) until you see *write a customer review*, and click on it.
- Next, you will be asked to sign in to Amazon. Insert your email address and Amazon password.
- If you don't already have an Amazon account, click on *Create your Amazon Account* (it's free) and follow the instructions.
- After you sign in, the *Create Review* page appears.
  - Overall rating: select the star on the far right to create a five-star review (please do not post any lower reviews).
  - Add a photo or video: skip this.
  - Add heading of your review: fill in or skip.
  - Write your review: fill in.
  - Click *submit*.
  - Great! Your review is complete.

Please send me a copy of your review to: gaskell11@outlook.com, so that I may use it in my book promotion. Thank you so much for your time and patience.

AFTERWORD

One year after you've read this book and implemented some of my advice, let me know how you're doing. Are you happy in the field of your choice? Are you successful in your own professional practice or business? Which of my advice worked best for you? Which of my counsel failed? What new items should I include in my next addition? If you didn't like the book, please tell me why. In any case, I wish you much continued success. Keep in touch.

And, if you haven't already done so, be sure to access your free bonus: "Starting Your Career" - Check List and "Your Marketing: - TOOL LIST. For free downloads go to: https://www.TheEngineersResource.com.

INDEX

APPENDIX

During the recent pandemic some businesses closed and didn't even modify their websites to indicate that fact. This certainly didn't garner them any good will. Others, like my local hardware store reduced hours, but again did not change their website and were closed when I arrived an hour before the usual closing time. I, like others, will seek a more reliable business to suit future needs.

Fortunately, many other businesses "stepped-up" and quickly modified their websites and practices to cope with the new reality. The following are some of the best examples that I was able to find on company websites. Perhaps, these will spark some ideas regarding your promotional needs. [Note: None of the businesses sited in this book have endorsed me or my book in any way and are not receiving compensation for the use.]

First, I decided to investigate businesses near my home here in North Palm Beach, Florida. In addition to the Pelican Café covered in Chapter 9, I discovered the following:

######

My favorite 'casual' Italian Restaurant: "Allora Pizza & Posta", at 420 US Hwy. One, North Palm beach, Florida 33408. They recently renovated with seating not only in the lovely dining room, but also outside in a spacious patio with large sun umbrellas. Tory and the other wait staff are friendly and efficient. Temporally, they are offering curbside pick-up and delivery only.

"Your neighborhood Italian"

The spread of Coronavirus (COVID-19) is on all of our minds. In order to keep serving and at the same time putting safety first we have adjusted our operation as follows and until further notice.

    We will be open for take-out and delivery only.

    Our working hours are 11am-9pm.

    We stop taking orders at 8:45pm. This will provide us with some extra time to sanitize all surfaces and equipment to safely serve you.

    If you feel more comfortable we will bring your order to your car. Just call us and let us know you're here and we will do the rest.

    We strongly encourage all our patrons to use our online ordering option at AlloraPizza.com where you can order and pay safely.

    Thank you for your patience and patronage.

Stay safe everyone!

######

Since I have been retired, I go to Planet Fitness Club every morning and work out for more than an hour. (9930 Alt AIA, Palm Beach Gardens, FL 33410 and 1222 Warwick Ave, Warwick, RI 02888.) I believe this is one of the reasons that I hardly ever have as ach or a pain. It gets me out of the house and helps me to keep a positive outlook. It is also one of the biggest bargains around. People at the club often comment on my many concert tee-shirts.

    Most of us enjoy music but attending a live concert is as *experience* and is one of my favorite things to do. My first concert was "Neil Diamond" and I think that he still holds the record of ten sold-out concerts in-a-row as Madison Square Garden. Unfortunately he is no longer touring due to Parkinson's disease. But, I checked the websites for my other favorites.

Elton John –   November 2 – London, GB – TICKETS AVAILABLE

Billy Joel –   June 6 – Madison Square Garden, NY – SOLD OUT

                 June 20 – Notre Dame, IN - TICKETS AVAILABLE

Kip Moore – July 10 Bangor, ME – TICKETS AVAILABLE

Zac Brown Band – Rescheduled to: – July 24 – Shakopee, MN – TICKETS AVAILABLE

I plan to be back in RI before July. I would enjoy a trip to Maine, if plans don't get "rescheduled".

######

Normally, after my workout at Planet Fitness each morning I visit my local Panera Bread for a great cup of iced coffee. My favorite cashier, Cathy always has a welcoming smile and remembers to greet me by name. I am always tempted by the cinnamon crisp bagels toasted with strawberry jelly & peanut butter on the side or the best orange scones in the world. And, I bring a book and often stay for lunch: creamy tomato soup – just like my mothers. I should give up coffee because I haven't had it since this nightmare began. But their iced tea might be a nice alternative.

Fortunately, they have been offering home/business delivery for about a year now so they had that up-and-running. But now they have added drive-up service and grocery delivery including things like milk and fruit.

Panera Bread Palm Beach Gardens - Northlake Boulevard
3186 Northlake Boulevard, Palm Beach Gardens, FL 33403
Phone: (561) 845-7747
About Panera Bread Palm Beach Gardens - Northlake Boulevard
panerabread.com

We believe that good clean food, food you can feel good about, brings out the best in all of us. Food served in our warm, welcoming fast-casual bakery-cafe, by people who care. At Panera Bread Palm Beach Gardens - Northlake Boulevard, that's good eating and that's why we're serving clean food without artificial preservatives, sweeteners, flavors or colors from artificial sources. And we're always finding new ways to make every soup, salad, sandwich and sweet bakery treat you eat at Panera the best (and cleanest) it can be. We're here to help when and where you need us.

Delivery - We deliver your Panera favorites right to your door with contactless delivery. Just tell us where to leave your meal in the "Delivery Instructions" box when placing your order. Plus get free delivery on every order of $15 or more through 4/30 with code FREEDELIVERY.*

Drive-Up - As part of our ongoing efforts to make sure your Panera experience is as safe as possible, we're introducing Panera Drive-Up. Now you can get your favorites to go without ever leaving your vehicle.

Panera Grocery - When you're cooking most of your meals at home, you may find yourself in need of a few grocery items to supplement bigger trips to the store. If you're lacking just a few ingredients—a loaf of bread, a gallon of milk, or an avocado here or there—there's no need to venture out to the store. Stay safe, stay in, and let Panera's pantry items help you fill in the gaps.

When I am here in Florida, I play in pool tournaments evenings on Mondays and Wednesdays At "Scooters Fun Food & Spirits", 8913 SE Bridge Road, Hobe Sound, Florida 33455. The entry fee for these tournaments is $5 and they pay out to four places. So, the sharks don't show up because even if they win the pot is small. But, some of the players are really good and I am not often in the money. Come to think of it, those guys are probably watching YouTube pool videos while I am finishing this book. I may never place again. I usually come to Scooters early because the food is good. They have the best chili any ware and on Wednesdays there is usually corn bread to go with it. And my favorite servers Cindy or Denise bring my food to the pool room.
    I checked out their website.

Scooters Fun Food & Spirits – We are open daily 10:30 am to 8:30 pm for takeout through the members door, curbside pickup, and local delivery.

I just ordered three bowls of chili with cheese for takeout. I will eat one bowl in the parking lot, put one in the fridge and another in the freezer.

######

When I bought my condo here in Florida, I purchased my furniture from ROOMS TO GO. They had a great selection and were willing to accept my order conditional upon the closing of my condo purchase and an uncertain delivery date. I found the following messages on their website.

Please check store pages for current showroom status.
Learn about our COVID-19 precautions here.

Free Doorway Delivery.

A great selection of in stock items on sale -
Delivered fast with minimal contact.

######

Most of the big chain stores have "stepped-up".

Here in Florida, I have always shopped at The Publix market nearby. I think it is great that they are opening early two mornings a week for seniors, first responders and hospital staff. The following new message appeared on the "Publix's" website:

Let's work together.

It's not always going to be perfect, but we'll get through this together:
WATCH NOW.

Publix is hear for you.

Latest updates.

Publix Super Markets Charities donates another $1 million to Feeding America member food banks.

This donation provides support to food pantries and meal programs in the communities surrounding Publix stores.

Publix offers extended hours for first responders and hospital staff.

Publix is designating Thursday evenings, 8 – 9 p.m., and Friday mornings, 7 – 8 a.m., as special shopping hours for first responders and hospital staff.

We've increased our social distancing measures.
We've put new measures in place to help protect our associates and our customers.

We're in this together.
Throughout our company Publix associates are working around the clock to best serve the evolving needs of our communities. Thank you for your patience and understanding if you experience limited inventory or delayed deliveries. And thank you for the kindness you have shown our associates working tirelessly to serve you.

Publix is here for you.

Adjusted Store Hours
We have adjusted the hours of all Publix locations to provide our store teams additional time to conduct preventive sanitation and to restock our shelves.

Learn How to Shop Online
Shop Publix right from your house using delivery or curbside pickup. Powered by Instacart. Here's a video tutorial to get you started.

Reserved Shopping Hours
We've designated special shopping hours for our customers age 65+. We've also reserved hours for first responders and hospital staff.

FAQs
Get answers to frequently asked questions that provide you more information about our stores during this situation.

Community Support
Publix and Publix Super Markets Charities are providing unprecedented support to our communities during these challenging times.

Customer Shopping Tips
From touch-free pay options to social distancing, here are some practical ways we can all look out for ourselves—and for others—in the checkout line.

Now Hiring
Publix is seeking to hire thousands of associates to fill positions in its stores and distribution centers.

Publix CEO Todd Jones
A Message From Our CEO
Todd Jones shares the actions Publix is taking to safeguard the health and well-being of our customers, associates, and communities.

######

I received the following message from a wonderful florist that I have used many times:

Pomfret Florists

Dear John,
First, I want to take a minute to reach out and thank our customers who have supported our business the past several weeks and especially Easter Week! Honestly, I didn't know if we would remain open during this crisis and our loyal customers answered the call and made it possible to keep going. Thank you all!

Second, going forward we will remain open, as long as it is safe to do so, however, our hours of operation will change.

Effective immediately - we will be open Monday through Saturday 9am to 3pm for local deliveries and pick-ups on the deck. Please call 508-678-6481 between these hours to place your order by phone or you can visit our website, www.pomfretflorist.com, 24/7.

Again, I can't express enough how critical your support has been the past few weeks. I know we spread happiness to everyone that we delivered flowers to.

Thank you,
David

We appreciate your business!
Pomfret Florists
836 County St
Somerset, Massachusetts 02726

pomfretflorist.com
CALL TODAY (508) 678-6481

######

I decided that I needed a paper cutter to assist with some of the mark-ups that I was creating for my book designer. I found a great selection of in-stock choices at Home Depot. At the top of their home page, I found the following message. Like others they didn't clutter their home page, but prominently offered the information. Next they offered discounts on things that people need when working from home.

Steps we are taking to help our customers & associates [Learn more]

50 % off on selected chairs

Enhance your working from home experience

Save $160 on selected PCs, monitors & printers

######

I decided to investigate what businesses were doing near my Rhode Island home in Pawtuxet Village, Rhode Island.
    I often entertained clients at BOSTA, an "up-scale" Italian restaurant.

BASTA Restaurant
Bosta's statement regarding COVIP - 19
We are in partial operation

The following statement popped-up on their menu page (A savvy way to expand their e-mail mailing list):

For a limited time, new subscribers will receive an email offering a free dessert for any dine-in order of $25 or more.

Email Address

Subscribe
We respect your privacy.

One of my favorite "Comfort Food" restaurants is now offering "take out". O'Rourke's Bar & Grill 23 Peck Lane & Narragansett Parkway, Warwick, RI - Even wine and "Family Style Meals – serving 4-6 people". I miss their Shepherd's Pie. This will be one of my first stops when I return to Rhode Island.

O'Rourke's Take Out Menu

We will now be offering Take-Out options. Please place your order by calling 401.228.7444. We will only be accepting credit cards (preferably when placing order) and will be allowing pick-up by using our side door with the ramp.

We also have beer & wine to go!
Open 1:00 pm-7:00 pm – Wed thru Sunday
New England Clam Chowder Cup – 4 Bowl – 8
Irish Nachos Half Order – 8   Full Order – 12
Quesadillas – 12   Add Chicken +2
Caesar Salad – 9   Add Chicken +4
Salmon Salad – 16
Gourmet Stuffed Quahogs –
1 for 4.50 or 2 for 8
Boneless Chicken Finger – 10
Pot Stickers with Teriyaki – 8

Pizza: Cheese & Pepperoni: – 10
add mushrooms, onion, peppers + .25 each
add chicken, sausage, or bacon +2 each

Corned Beef Sandwich – 10
Tuna Melt – 10.50
Corned Beef Reuben – 11 "House Favorite!"
Fresh "not frozen" Burger – 10

Chicken Caesar Wrap – 10
Hot Dog 1 for 7 or 2 for 9
Fish Taco's – 10
Turkey Club – 12
Guinness Battered
Fish and Chips with Cole Slaw – 13
Baked Scrod w/ Mashed Potato – 14
Shephard's Pie – 11
Penna al la Vodka with Grilled Chicken – 14

PLEASE CALL
HOURS IN ADVANCE
FOR FAMILY STYLE MEALS
FAMILY STYLE MEALS : (serves 4-6) – $30 each
Chicken Marsala –
served with choice of
penne or mashed potato,

Chicken Francoise – served
with penne or mashed potato

Pasta & Meatballs

Chicken Parmesan w penne

Penne al la Vodka with Chicken

Recently, I celebrated my 78th birthday here in Florida. On previous years, I have returned to Rhode Island to spend our birthday with my twin sister. But, unfortunately she has passed away. Now with this pandemic, I am stuck here alone and socially distancing. But, I was "cheered" by the prospect of curb-side-pick-up at Red Lobster, 2201 Palm Beach Lakes Blvd., West Palm Beach, FL 33409.

When I went to the website I was encouraged by the heading on the home page:

"West Palm Beach (Delivery Available)".

At the top of the Menu page was the following statement:

"It's our promise that all of the food we serve is sourced to the highest standards. Due to supply disruptions we are currently offering a limited To Go menu; some substitutions may apply. Thank you for your understanding."

There were a lot of mouthwatering choices but I finally chose the following for my birthday dinner:

'Lobster Lovers Dream'
"A succulent roasted rock lobster tail, butter-pouched Main lobster tail, and lobster-and-shrimp linguini Alfaro. Served with chose of sides (and including Cheddar Bay Biscuits). Available while it lasts."

I Phoned in my order and called again when I arrived. A pretty gal came out and passed my meal through the open driver's side window and placed it gently on the seat. (I didn't really need the face mask & gloves that I was wearing.)

It wasn't really hot when I got it home but I didn't take the tine to re-heat it. It smelled wonderful and it was delicious!!!!!

######

I get all of my prescriptions filled at my local CVS, both in RI and in FL. I do this because of the knowledgeable and friendly service and great products, but also I am pleased to support a Rhode Island based company.

I went to the CVS Health homepage and it included the following:

We are closely monitoring the COVID-19 outbreak and are in regular contact with health officials. Here is what you need to know:

Rapid COVID-19 testing locations open
With federal and state officials, CVS Health opens drive-through testing sites in
Connecticut, Georgia, Massachusetts and Rhode Island.

Protecting and supporting customers and our employees.
We've made changes in our stores and are providing extra employee benefits.

Responding to the pandemic:
CVS Health will hire 50,000 people, provide bonuses and additional benefits to
existing workers.

Insights:
Health Trends 2020
In our constantly changing industry, here are the developments we believe are
worth watching in the year ahead, and the related work we're doing to help people
on their path to better health.

How we're focused on you:
Cost of care
We've developed solutions to help patients save on their prescription drugs and
more easily access affordable and efficient care.

$100 M committed to improving community health nationwide through Building
Healthier Communities.

######

All of my books have been sold on "Amazon". They recently bought my printer
'Create Space' and Amazon.com is the "world's largest bookstore". They began
by selling books from their website in 1995, and are now the world's largest
online retailer of consumer goods. Because of my books, I visit their website
often. On a recent visit I found the following:

AMAZON AND COVID – 19
We are giving priority to essential items that our customers need the most. You
may experience shipping delays. Learn more on COVID – 19

Amazon is focused on the health and safety of our associates and based on regional regulations and social distancing requirements this has resulted in extended response times. We ask for your patience in this challenging time as our teams work to deliver this vital service to customers everywhere, especially to those, like the elderly, who are most vulnerable.

Find answers to how orders and deliveries are affected by COVID-19 here. Many of your inquiries can be self-served through our Help resources. You can track your orders and deliveries, return a product, manage your Prime account, and get help for your Amazon devices.

We apologize for the inconvenience.

######

A few weeks ago I ran out of copy paper and as an author I use a lot of paper. My local Staples was offering 1 hour pick-up, but I decided to order delivery. It was 11:30 am and the free delivery date promised was the next day. And, sure enough it showed-up the next morning at 10 am. I had ordered an 8 ream box for less than $25. The box was so heavy that I couldn't lift it. So, I opened it on my porch and took in two reams at a time. Staples has always come through for me. Their website offered the following.

On the Home page: A message to our valued customers from CEO, Sandy Douglas. (Read More)

The first thing that I noticed is that they didn't clutter up the home page with a lengthy message, but the reader could select (Read More) if they chose. When I selected it, a new page opened with first a summery followed by details.

Staples CEO Update: Employee Safety, Free Shipping & No Minimums and Managing High-Demand Items.

Back to the home page, I found that they were offering a discount coupon with is a good idea under normal conditions, but very generous under these special circumstances.

$20 off your online order of $100 or more.

A few days after my recent order from Staples, I received an e-mail.

"Tips for the times"
This spring isn't going the way you or your high school junior expected. But you can still prepare (and get excited) for the process of applying to college with these tips. [Link]

I was expecting when I clicked on the link it would try to sell me a College Prep Course. But instead it revealed a helpful article. The same applied to the other links. This was actually a message to help customers – not to sell to them products. Hat's off to Staples. Also included were the following:

Test Tip
Tour Tip
Essay Tip
5 Things to do now

######

I like cruses mostly because they offer a relaxing vacation with many optional activities and always the alternative to easily return to my stateroom. I started traveling with Norwegian because of their flexible dining options. I continued because of their friendly staff and the grand but relaxing atmosphere. My first cruise after retiring started on the west coast of South America, went through the Panama Canal and disembarked in Boston. (As we passed through the canal, I learned a palindrome: "A man a plan a canal Panama".) Last summer I took both grandchildren to Hawaii and took a cruise around the islands on the Norwegian's "Pride of America". We had an aft facing stateroom with a huge balcony including two chairs, two lounges and room to walk around.

    After reading about the current bargains, I am seriously considering booking a cruise for next year. Even if I choose to wear a face mask it would be great to go on vacation and see some interesting places.

TRAVEL ALERT Updated: April 24, 2020 - Suspended cruises into June 2020
Cruses From $199

Free Open Bar
Free Specialty Dining
Free Excursions
Free WIFI
Free Kids
Book with NORWEGIAS'S PEACE of MIND
And change plans as needed

######

A few years ago I did several home exchanges. There are many websites offering to connect like-minded people. Some people express concerns with this concept, but it has always worked out well for me. All of my exchanges were non-simultaneous, which means I used their property and they later used mine.

This is often the case when both parties have a second home. My destinations included Narbonne, France; Verona, Italy; Vancouver, British Columba; Seattle, Washington; and Acapulco, Mexico. Some even provided a car exchange. The website that I used was "Home for Exchange". They offer thousands of properties from all over the world and the cost currently is $8-$12 per month with a two week trial period and you can view all of the properties before you join.

I checked out their website and found no corvid warning.

A nice condo in North Palm Beach, Florida – with no availability.

A modern condo in South Beach Miami, Florida with a spectacular view– with no availability.

A home in Seattle, Washington with a magnificent view of the down-town – with availability next week and most of next month. **But, I don't know if they are actually taking bookings.**

######

NOTES

Purchase additional copies of this book at a *discount*.
Go to: https://www.TheEngineersResource.com.
Enter coupon code: paperback

NOTES